# Wake Up and Join the Evolution

### How To Create a world of peace, prosperity and happiness

Sandra Weaver

**BALBOA**
PRESS

A DIVISION OF HAY HOUSE

Balboa Press books may be ordered through booksellers or by contacting:

Balboa Press
A Division of Hay House
1663 Liberty Drive
Bloomington, IN 47403
www.balboapress.com
1-(877) 407-4847

Because of the dynamic nature of the Internet, any web addresses or links contained in this book may have changed since publication and may no longer be valid. The views expressed in this work are solely those of the author and do not necessarily reflect the views of the publisher, and the publisher hereby disclaims any responsibility for them.

The author of this book does not dispense medical advice or prescribe the use of any technique as a form of treatment for physical, emotional, or medical problems without the advice of a physician, either directly or indirectly. The intent of the author is only to offer information of a general nature to help you in your quest for emotional and spiritual well-being. In the event you use any of the information in this book for yourself, which is your constitutional right, the author and the publisher assume no responsibility for your actions.

Any people depicted in stock imagery provided by Thinkstock are models, and such images are being used for illustrative purposes only. Certain stock imagery © Thinkstock.

ISBN: 978-1-4525-5084-8 (sc)
ISBN: 978-1-4525-5085-5 (e)

Library of Congress Control Number: 2012907954

Printed in the United States of America

Balboa Press rev. date: 5/17/2012

# *Preface*

Have you ever felt so certain and been so excited about something that you felt the need to tell everyone? This is how I felt after reading numerous books about the Mayan calendar and the predictions for the year 2012. The more I read, the more I wanted to "tell the world" about this once-in-a-lifetime opportunity we, living on this planet today, have to create a world of peace and plenty for all. Many of the books that I have read have been written by scholars of the Mayan calendar. Some of them have been authored by scientists, physicists, biologists and other professionals. Still others are people who have studied the evolution of our culture for many years. It is important to understand that while December 21, 2012 does mark the end of a 5125 year era and the beginning of a new world age, that is only part of the story. For years, there have been many individuals and groups working to make our world a safer, friendlier and more peaceful place in which to live. Today it is time for *all* of us to wake up and take an active role in this new Evolution.

I have always believed it was possible for human beings to live in peace with one another. It is our nature to be friendly and helpful to those around us whether we know them or not. What gets in the way of truly connecting with people is our insistence that our way of thinking is the "right" way. Therefore, we choose not to interact with those who hold differing beliefs. There are those who think that all of the hype about 2012 is just that…hype. They purport that global warming is just a cycle and poses no real danger to the planet. Some even believe it is a "scam". There are those who believe that 2012 will be the end of the world and Judgment Day. They believe we will experience horrendous disasters as "punishment" for our sinful ways. Some people have never even heard of 2012 or, if they have, just haven't given it a second thought.

This is why I was inspired to write this book. I want to share what I have learned, but more importantly, I want to encourage my readers to discover these truths for themselves. I wrote this book for a specific audience. They are as follows:

- Those people who have never heard of anything exceptional happening in 2012
- Those people who believe that 2012 is the end of the world and only those true believers will be saved
- Those people that laugh and snicker at the "woo woo" that is being talked about with regard to 2012.
- Those people who are set in their beliefs and consider day-to-day events "just the way life is".

It is also written for the choir: those people who know what is happening and the challenges and opportunities it presents. It is my hope that those people will pass the book on to their family, co-workers, friends and neighbors who might be willing to spend just an hour of their day reading it.

I have presented the scientific facts in an easy to understand language with the hope that you will be as intrigued as I was and want to learn more. I have included references to authors, organizations, websites and scientific data which I hope will peak your curiosity and compel you to do some research of your own. I also share my own thoughts on what we on planet earth have created up to now, and what might be possible as we move into the next 5125 year cycle which will begin on December 22, 2012.

The first book I read was *The Mystery of 2012* which is a compilation of essays by a number of authors. One of them, Gregg Braden, especially captured my attention. Gregg is a former Senior Computer Systems Designer for Martin Marietta Aerospace and Computer Geologist for Phillips Petroleum and the first Technical Operations Manager for Cisco Systems. He has searched the remote monasteries of Egypt, Peru and Tibet for the life-giving secrets that were encoded in the language of our most cherished traditions, the wisdom of which he believes is the key to our future. I became fascinated with Gregg's study of the Mayans, their calendar, and the end of a 5125 year cycle. I went on to read other books by Gregg Braden including *Fractal Time* and *The Divine Matrix*. I also have had the opportunity to hear him speak.

At a Hay House Conference in California, I had the opportunity to hear Bruce Lipton speak. Bruce is the other of *The Biology of Belief* and co-author of *Spontaneous Evolution*. He is an internationally recognized authority in bridging science and spirit and a leading voice in new biology. A cell biologist by training, he taught at the University of Wisconsin's School of Medicine and later performed pioneering studies at Stanford University. His work met with skepticism by his peers at first, but later proved to be indisputable. Dr. Lipton compares the cells in our body with individuals in a community and shows us how, by working together as our cells do, we can create a healthy and peaceful environment for humanity. There is much more, but I leave that to you to read for yourself.

I have learned how powerful our hearts are through the work of Howard Martin and organizations like Heart Math. When groups of people collaborate to send coherent heart care to areas of unrest or suffering, it can help to reduce that suffering. The

Global Coherence Monitoring System is being developed to further study this phenomena. Through the Shift Network, I was able to hear speakers like Barbara Marx Hubbard, Jean Houston, Marianne Williamson, Lynn McTaggart, Gregg Braden, Bruce Lipton, Howard Martin, Neale Donald Walsh and many others.

This book is not about a year or a specific date in history as much as it is about the amazing Universe in which we live. It is about the magnetism of the earth and how we are connected to it and to every other being on the planet. It is about how we are interacting with *all* life on Earth and the outcome of that interaction. It is about becoming aware of our beliefs and whether they are still true today. It is an invitation to look at the world we have created and decide whether there might be a better way of living. Most importantly, it is a wake-up call for everyone living on the planet today. You are the chosen ones. You are here for a reason. It is *you,* in cooperation with your fellow "Earthians" who will determine the future of our lives here on planet Earth.

# The Mayan Mystery

Much has been written about the Mayan calendar and its predictions for the year 2012. The responses to these phenomena have ranged from those predicting it will be the end of the world to spiritual teachers who believe it will be the beginning of an era of peace and prosperity. As you are reading this book, we are well into the year 2012 and perhaps beyond. On the surface, it may seem that we are nowhere near an era of peace and prosperity. However, there are grass roots movements in many areas that could create a shift to turn us away from war, selfishness and greed towards harmony, love and the birth of a new humanity.

The Mayans measured time in cycles. The Maya "Great Cycle" equals 5125 years. It began on August 11, 3114 BC and will end on December 21, 2012AD at which time a new cycle begins. So, to put it in basic terms, 2012 is the end of one cycle and the beginning of another. The Maya considered the Great Cycle to be one world age, one growth cycle, at the end of which, humanity reaches the next stage in its spiritual development. They did not say it would be the end of the world.

The facts as we know them from archeological records show that the first Maya appeared over a millennium and a half ago in remote areas which are now in Mexico's Yucatan Peninsula, Guatemala, Honduras, and Belize. They appear to have arrived with advanced technology already in place. One of the most amazing discoveries was their exact calculation of cosmic cycles. In addition to tracking familiar solar and lunar cycles, the 5000 year old Mayan calendar also seemed to track a rare celestial alignment of our solar system, our sun and our planet aligning with the center of our galaxy. This event happens every 26,000 years.

This alignment is known as the Precessional cycle and was calculated and plotted in the Mayan calendars. The Earth's precession of the equinoxes cycle takes nearly 26,000 years to complete. It is the result of the Earth wobbling as it turns on its axis during its twenty-four hour orbit around the sun. There is a relationship between this and galactic synchronization: an astronomical event that will bring the Earth and the planets of the solar system into an alignment with a central point in the Milky Way. The next 26,000 year alignment will happen on December 21, 2012. The Maya related the 260 day sacred cycle (our human gestation period) to the 26,000 year cycle as our collective gestation, our unfolding as a species.

Jose Arguelles is one of the leaders in the field of modern Mayan calendar predictions. He is the author of the book, "The Mayan Factor". He describes his meeting with a Maya by the name of Hunbatz Men who told him that our star system represents the seventh star system that the Maya have mapped, charted and navigated. In his studies, Arguelles determined that the Great Cycle isn't so much a measurement of time as it is the measurement of this planet's passage through a beam that is 5,125 years wide. Earth has been passing through this beam since 3113 BC. According to the Mayan calendar, we will depart from that beam in 2012. While all of the planets are passing through this beam, the passing is expected to have particular meaning for planet Earth. Arguelles compares this beam to a wave that has been building up for 5100 years and is about to break. The breaking point of the wave occurred on August 16 and 17, 1987 and was known as the Harmonic Convergence, named for the world's first globally synchronized meditation. According to Arguelles, this would mark a new age of universal peace. There are other prophecies and writings about the Harmonic Convergence which can be easily accessed via the internet.

What sets the Mayan prophecy apart from the general predictions of other cultures is that is has an expiration date that occurs in our lifetime. The last cycle of the Mayan calendar corresponds to a series of tangible events, some of which are happening today. Here is what we know for certain: 1) the end of the Mayan great Cycle marks a rare alignment of our planet, our solar system, and the center of our galaxy, one that will not occur again for another 26,000 years. 2) On March 10, 2006 a cycle of solar storms ended and a new cycle began. It is predicted to peak in 2012, with an intensity30-50-percent greater than previous cycles. (this is already occurring) 3) Scientists agree that Earth's magnetic fields are weakening quickly and some suspect that we are in the early stage of a polar reversal. While we have always thought of the magnetic fields of our planet as a certainty (the needle of a compass always points north), they are not. Every once in a while our familiar North and South poles trade places...the magnetic field of the earth does a flip flop. While these are rare, they have happened 171 times in the last 76 million years. The symptoms of these flip flops are abrupt changes in weather patterns and a rapid weakening of the planet's magnetic field, both of which are happening right now. 4) Earth's magnetics play a key role in how we accept new ideas and change in our lives. All life is strongly influenced by magnetic changes. The human brain contains millions of tiny magnetic particles and connects us to the earth's magnetic field in a powerful way. Thus, if the earth's magnetic fields are changing, we too are affected. Scientists in the twentieth century learned, through looking at the strength of magnetic ribbon-like patterns across the planet, that places with stronger magnetic fields hold more traditional beliefs whereas, in places where the fields are weaker, people are more open to change. It probably comes as no surprise that one of the areas of lowest magnetism is the West Coast of the United States. California has always been known as a "trend setter".

One of the most visible changes that we are seeing is climate. We are experiencing global warming and dramatic deviations in our weather patterns. This has great implications for our future. Science has shown us that we are not the cause of these changes. The planet's position in space creates patterns of warming and cooling that repeat on a cyclical basis. However, this is a time when the people of this planet must work together to share resources and ideas, and to adapt to the changes that are beyond our control. What does climate change have to do with the way we are governed or the way that we live? It simply means that we have to become aware of what is happening on our planet, how it is affecting our way of life and take steps to adapt to the changing conditions.

Gregg Braden has studied the Mayan calendar, and has searched the remote monasteries of Egypt, Peru and Tibet for the live-giving secrets that were encoded in the language of our most cherished traditions. He has learned much from our indigenous ancestors and from the Mayan elders. They knew this time was coming. What they do not know is whether we can adapt to the changes and embrace the fact that we are a world family and possibly part of a greater cosmic family. Gregg Braden was a major inspiration for the writing of this book, and a listing of his books is included in the reference section.

As we enter this period of change, the systems that we have in place are challenged. Those that have proven to be sustainable will continue; those that are not will collapse. When we look at our economic system, monetary system, health care and even the way our government is run, it's pretty easy to see that they are not working optimally. Never in the history of our planet, have we been faced with so many crises of such great magnitude. Our first inclination has always been to solve the problem by finding someone or something to blame, replacing him, her or it and continuing on the same path. Albert Einstein defined insanity as "Doing the same thing over and over and expecting different results". We will not be able to solve our present crises with the same thinking that created them. Does that mean we must be out of our mind in order to solve our problems? Probably. Will it be easy? Probably not. This is a window of opportunity to change our thinking and ways of being. It will be up to those of us living on the planet today to respond to the crises and do what is necessary to sustain a high quality of life for everyone. Our biggest challenge will be our willingness to change our beliefs.

# *Beliefs*

The key to saving our planet, our civilization and our lives is to challenge our beliefs. How do we do that? We can change the way we believe if we take a look at the beliefs we hold and where they came from. Then, just for a moment, entertain the idea that they may not be true today. Most of what we believe we have learned from our parents, teachers and spiritual leaders. This gave us our guide as to what was right or wrong, true or false. We have been living with them for centuries as each generation passed them on to the next. The beliefs that we have held in the past seemed to have served us well, and we have been doing the best we know how. Now, with scientific facts staring us in the face, we need to re-think many of our old beliefs. This will not be easy. Even scientists have had to admit that some of what they had previously believed was an undeniable fact has been proven to be false.

One of those scientists is Bruce Lipton. Dr. Lipton is a pioneer in new biology and an internationally recognized leader in bridging science and spirit. As a cell biologist, his work focused on mechanisms through which energy in the form of beliefs can affect our biology including our genetic code. While we have always believed that our "genes" are the reason for much of our behavior, addictions and health issues, scientists have now discovered this is not true. Dr. Lipton discovered that the cell membrane, not the nucleus, is actually the "brain" of the cell. The membrane responds to its environment and behaves accordingly. This means that life experiences can actively redefine our genetic traits. Our perceptions not only control our behavior, but also control gene activity. A new branch of science called Epigenetics reveals that we are not victims, but masters of our genes. Refer to Dr. Bruce Lipton's book: *Spontaneous Evolution* in the reference section.

Another scientist, Gregg Braden, a major inspiration for this book, has discovered many long-held beliefs that have been proven to be false. Gregg has studied the Mayan culture and calendar, and has spoken with the indigenous people about their prophecies for the future. He has discovered that life on our planet is much older than we have believed. Up until now, it was believed that life on our planet was just 5000 years old. New discoveries, however, have now proven that life on this planet began long before that. Gregg Braden has been researching this ancient history, and has visited the sites of many civilizations no longer in existence. He has learned much from our indigenous ancestors and from the Mayan elders. His most recent book, *Deep Truth* offers scientific facts and what they mean for us living on earth today.

Going way back, the common belief was that the world was flat. That was the truth. Then it was discovered that the world was not flat, but round. There are many scientific "facts" that have now been proven untrue. In *Deep Truth* Gregg Braden tells us that it is necessary to recognize when a truth that has been thought to be undeniable is proven incorrect. We must then acknowledge the new truth and act from it. Unfortunately, our textbooks and school curricula continue to teach the flawed information.

## Examining our beliefs

What are the beliefs you hold that you deem to be the absolute truth? Are there beliefs concerning God, religion, government, politics, environment, education, health, physics, family, marriage or other areas to which you hold fast? Would you be willing to change those beliefs if it were proven to you that they were *not* true? How would that affect your behavior or way of living? Would it frighten you or excite you?

If scientists who have long held proven beliefs can, with new information and discoveries, accept that those beliefs are no longer true and move forward with that information, should not we be able to at least consider re-thinking our beliefs? Based on the beliefs we have been taught, we have created our system of government, education, health care, environmental management and business practices. How's that working for us today? Let's take a look at our current systems.

# *Energy and the Environment*

Let's begin by talking about energy with regard to our bodies. Energy is vital to our existence and to maintain the life of our bodies. That energy is used for growth and for protection. When the energy is used for growth, our bodily functions operate at optimal performance resulting in a healthy human being. When energy is used for protection, it takes away some energy that could be used for growth. Protection mechanisms are necessary for our wellbeing, particularly in fighting off disease. Protection energy is also used when a person is suffering from stress or fear. Twenty-five percent of the energy in our body is used by our brain. Our thoughts use energy. Whenever we have a thought of worry or fear, we are taking away the energy that could be used for growth. When we expend our energy by worrying about whether we might contract a disease in the future or if we might get the flu this season, our growth energy is diminished. With the media putting us on terror alerts and the military gearing up to "keep us safe", we are way out of balance in our growth vs. protection energy.

We need to become aware of how we are using our thoughts, and whether they are contributing to our growth or being used up for protection. When we entertain thoughts of how bad the world is or how dangerous it is, we are expending energy which could be used for growth. In addition, because our thoughts create a vibration, they can bring back to us exactly what we are thinking.

The world as we know it runs on energy. Energy is vital to life on this planet. We derive much of our energy from environmental resources such as the sun, the ocean and the earth. Prior to the evolution of human beings, organisms relied on renewable resources for survival. Humans, in their technological advances, began to use non-renewable resources with the belief that there would always be enough. The fallacy in that belief is staring us in the face at this moment. We now know that depletion of resources and fossil fuel technology are not sustainable for another millennium.

If we do not change the way we live, it is highly likely that we will become extinct. Our planet has experienced five extinctions in its lifetime and scientists believe we are into our sixth. Really? Could life on planet Earth, including we humans, actually become extinct? Extinction is the result of animals or plants being unable to adapt to changing conditions. They fail to manage life's energy. The first four extinctions were caused by climate change; the fifth by a collision between earth and extra- terrestrial bolide (cometary) or possibly a great volcanic event. The sixth extinction will be the only one caused by human beings. How are we causing this? We pollute our air and water to the point of endangering human and animal life. We continue to destroy many species as we disrupt the vital functioning of ecosystems on which all life depends. We deplete the non-renewable resources that are so vital for life. The result: extinction of life on planet Earth. Gregg Braden says, in the introduction of his book *Deep Truth*: "It's not Earth that's in trouble. It's us, the people who *live* here on Earth. I can say with a high degree of confidence that our planet will still be here 50 years from now, and 500 years from now. No matter what choices we make during that time period – no matter how many wars we wage, and how many political revolutions we begin or how badly we pollute our air and oceans – the world that our ancestors called the "garden" will still be here making the same 365.256-day journey around the sun each year, just as it has for the past 4.55 billion years or so. The question is not about Earth; it's about whether or not we will be *on* Earth to enjoy it."

John Petersen, president of The Arlington Institute, is considered by many to be one of the most informed futurists in the world. His essay in the book: *The Mystery of 2012* addresses natural resources, species extinction, climate change, economic ramifications and the necessity for a new way of living. He notes a study which shows that the ocean's fish are being depleted so rapidly that in a mere forty years, eating seafood may become just a memory.

Global warming has become a controversial subject. There are those who proclaim that it is just a cycle, that it has happened before and is no big deal. They are correct in that it is a cycle. Climate change has been occurring in a cyclical manner for thousands of years. The planet's position in space creates patterns of warming and cooling that repeat on a cyclical basis. We did not cause it but, due to the number of people living on the planet today, we are exacerbating it. Consider this: In 1804, there were one billion people on earth. One hundred and twenty three years later, we grew to two billion and continued to grow by billions in a shorter and shorter period of time. Today, in 2012, we are now at seven billion folks. So you can see that, while we are experiencing just another cycle of climate change which we did not cause, our responsibility is to learn how to adapt to those changes and adjust our behavior so as to be in harmony with it. Our survival depends on it. The fact is that Earth is now as warm as at any time in the last 10,000 years and within 1degree C of being the hottest it has been in a million years. John Petersen gives many more examples and documentations in that essay. The book is listed in the reference section.

Although it seems our leaders are oblivious to the destruction we are causing our environment, President Obama has created the first ever Ocean Stewardship Policy. The Executive Order #13547 establishes a national policy to ensure the protection, maintenance and restoration of the health of the ocean, coastal and great lakes ecosystems and resources. To read the full order go to www.whitehouse.gov/the-pres-office/executive -ord.

Most of us have grown up with the idea that there is always enough, and that there is more where that came from. The most glaring example of that is the way we have used our non-renewable resources. The safety of our food and water is at stake as well. When the oceans are polluted it affects the fish we eat. Pesticides and the way our animals are fed and raised is also a concern. **Food and Water Watch** is a non-profit organization that advocates for common sense policies that will result in healthy, safe food and access to safe and affordable drinking water. You can learn more about them at www.foodandwaterwatch.org

Another organization that is actively working to protect our valuable resources is the **Worldwatch Institute.** Founded in 1974 by farmer and economist, Lester Brown, Worldwatch was the first independent research institute dedicated to the analysis of global environmental concerns. Now, under the leadership of population expert and author, Robert Engelman, Worldwatch develops innovative solutions to difficult problems, emphasizing a blend of government leadership, private sector enterprise and citizen action that can make a sustainable future a reality.

We know we need to become less dependent on oil and find other sources of energy. Yet we continue off-shore drilling despite the devastation we have seen as a result of the recent tragic oil spills. We realize we are permanently harming our environment, but we are unwilling to give up our dependence on oil. This is evidenced by the fact that even after the horrendous BP oil spill and the death and devastation of our sea life and beaches, our Government has given the go-ahead for more off shore drilling. We continue to hold the belief that it won't happen again or that the gain far outweighs the risk. We simply don't get that we need to find another source of energy. Well, many folks do get it, and they need to have their voices heard by the powers that be.

We have become dependent upon oil to the degree that we are dependent upon other nations to provide for that need. There are more inexpensive ways to provide energy, but, just as the pharmaceutical industry does not promote holistic healing, the oil companies turn a blind eye to other sources of energy. Now, with the stark reality of diminishing supplies and the unrest among countries who supply this precious resource, we need to reconsider other ways of providing the energy on which we have become so dependent. We also need to recognize that we cannot continue to use non-renewable resources if we want to survive on this planet. And, since this planet is the only home we know at this juncture, we need to wake up to this reality.

Even though there is increased awareness that our oil resources are finite, demand for oil is growing, driven by the needs of China and India. Supply, on the other hand, has peaked. Production of 84 million barrels a day has remained steady while the demand exceeds that. Oil importers are looking to oil rich, yet underdeveloped countries to meet their demands. At this time, they have used economic and political means to compete for oil, but as the supply peaks, might they resort to military strategies?

# *Government*

Our founding fathers envisioned a government OF the people, BY the people and FOR the people. They knew that if the commonwealth were to survive, the power must be held by the people. What does that mean? It means that we, the people, ARE the government regardless of who holds the office of President. It is our responsibility to hold our elected officials accountable in assuring a country where all citizens enjoy life, liberty and the pursuit of happiness. How are we doing? If we look at the violence in our homes, schools and on our streets, the imbalance of wealth in our nation, children going to bed hungry and others living on the street, we can see we have a lot of work to do.

Our founding fathers did an amazing job in building the foundation for our way of governing. But our two party system is beginning to crumble. We have the Democrats and the Republicans, each with their own beliefs of how this nation should be run. Instead of working together for the greater common good, our legislators seem to be only out for themselves and their re-election. When a bill is introduced by a Republican, you can be fairly confident that most Democrats will oppose it. The opposite is also true. The result is that nothing gets done. There is more action in their campaigns for election or re-election than there is on the floor of Congress. Do we need to re-think a two party system? There have been a few attempts to create a viable third party, but none have been successful. There was even an attempt to create a party where the President and Vice President would be of two different parties. That idea fell by the wayside as well.

What happened to compromise? While we have always thought of compromise as a viable solution to a problem, there is a better way. Synthesis is a process whereby the best in both liberal and conservative perspectives is highlighted on an issue to create more innovative policies. We may have seen a glimmer of this happening when Congress was in a heated and contentious debate over raising the debt ceiling. They did eventually come to a compromised solution, and the components of that compromise included ideas that both parties espoused. If we look at a different way of achieving compromise, it might be that each party in a dispute would offer what they believed to be the greatest benefits of their position. These would be put on the table and the ideas that both parties held would be a place to begin. An activity that some debate classes use is to have each side argue for the position to which they are opposed and vice versa. We cannot continue to do what we have always done to solve problems and expect different results. We are born with a creative mind. Let's learn how to use it.

Although it seems we cannot seem to make a dent in our flawed political system, there is hope. While our two-party system seems to provide nothing but dissention and disagreement, Corrine McLaughlin believes that the increased power of the Independent sector will be seen as the new superpower by 2012. It has neither a set of beliefs nor any identified leader. Its power is based on ideas rather than force. According to an exit poll by Zogby International, poverty and economic justice topped the list of the most urgent moral problems in American culture rather than issues such as abortion or same-sex marriage. This is just another indication that spiritual values will drive the face of politics in the future. Today, according to a Zogby Poll, one in four voters supports a third party or an Independent candidate. Breaking it down demographically, 41% of those voters are 18-29 years of age and 36% are independents. Our youth will lead the way!

# *Economics and Finance*

We have certainly seen a breakdown in our financial system to the point of corruption. Businesses are ruled by the "bottom line" which is profit. That may mean cutting corners on manufacturing or raising retail prices. Corporations are beholden to their shareholders. In order to assure the greatest return to their investors, the corporations also see profit as their highest priority. Goods are produced at the lowest cost by outsourcing labor to countries who will work cheaper. The result: less jobs for Americans and often poorer quality products. Of course, if a product's life is short, there will be more need to replace the item sooner resulting in more money for the company.

The goal of making money has led to corruption, greed and devastation of many lives in our recent history. We are operating on the survival of the fittest mentality and the idea that we must get or accumulate as much as we can. We have been taught that bigger and more are better, and that **competition** is the way for us to win and get to the top! This is the economic principle we have been living. We must change to a humanitarian principle where the good of the people trumps the wealth of the corporations.

Bruce Lipton, in comparing humans with cells notes one difference between successful cellular economics and the failing human economy. He says that when cells assembled into communal life forms, the economic emphasis was not on the wealth of the individuals, but on the well-being of the collective, the shared wealth of all. When human beings realize they are just one cell in the body of *humanity*, they will see cooperation as the way to create a world and life that works for everyone. This is collective intelligence.

There is hope in the business community. I refer again to Corrine McLaughlin, author of *Spiritual Politics* and *The Builders of the Dawn*, which show us how Spirituality and consciousness are at work in our business communities. She writes that the "hottest buzz" today is the idea of a "triple bottom line", a commitment to people, planet and profit." Corrine has been active in the International Spirit at Work organization and a fellow of the World Business Academy which promotes corporate responsibility. Business for Social Responsibility (BSR) is a San Francisco-based nonprofit founded in the 1990's and has grown to encompass over 400 organizations, including about half of the Fortune 500 companies. BSR defines corporate social responsibility as a "comprehensive set of policies, practices and programs" that earn financial success in ways that "honor ethical values and respect people, communities and the natural environment." Many companies now hold meditation classes and Apple Computer's California offices have a dedicated meditation room where employees may spend a half hour a day on company time to meditate, pray or just sit in silence. This has proven to improve employee productivity and creativity.

The World Business Academy, founded by Rinaldo Brutoco, is a non-profit business think tank and network of business and thought leaders. It was founded in 1986 with the mission to inspire and help businesses assume responsibility for the whole of society with relation to critical, moral, environmental and social dilemmas. The Academy's work and extensive publications address the challenges of innovative and values-driven leadership, renewable energy and climate change, development of the human potential at work, sustainable business strategies and global reconstruction. Visit their website at www. worldbusiness.org.

Another organization working to eliminate abusive financial practices is the Center for Responsible Lending (CRL). It is affiliated with Self-Help, a community development lender, credit union and Real Estate developer that works with individuals, organizations and communities traditionally underserved by conventional markets.

Can we maintain our freedom to pursue financial gain and still be conscious of the needs of others? It is possible and it is already happening. Bill and Melinda Gates are widely recognized for their philanthropic gifts to fight poverty and improve health and education around the world. Warren Buffet has donated most of his fortune to the Gates foundation. George Soros has contributed 50 million dollars to fight AIDS and poverty in Africa. Richard Branson of the Virgin Group has given 3 billion from the Virgin's train and airline business to fight global warming. There are many more wealthy individuals and foundations donating large sums of money for worthy causes.

Money is energy. Money has power. You don't need to be a millionaire or a large corporation to use the power of your money. You can make a difference and contribute to positive change on our planet. There are many local organizations that are feeding the hungry, sheltering the homeless and those being abused by domestic violence, and contributing in many other ways to make their community a better place. Your contribution of just a few dollars or, even more importantly, your contribution of time to these organizations as a volunteer will have a positive impact.

Conversely, *not* spending your money can wield power as well. When we do not spend our money with companies who are not environmentally friendly or who do not treat their employees well, it affects their bottom line. If we do not support the advertisers of a TV program that we find offensive, it can affect both the advertiser and the producer of the TV show. Money talks. What is your money saying?

Creating abundance on our planet is as simple as this: take care of one another in your own families and neighborhoods. Many of our neighborhoods have a "neighborhood watch". This was designed to keep neighborhoods safe from crime and vandalism. What if, in addition, neighborhood watch kept an eye out for people in need and reached out to help those people? Think about the implications of this kind of practice. The Government is spending billions of dollars on social programs to help those who need assistance in obtaining food, clothing and shelter. If we each took care of a neighbor in need, we could cut that spending considerably. There is a story told about a man who noticed two rooms of people sitting at a table with food in front of them. In one room, the people were starving yet in another they were laughing and enjoying their meal. When he looked closer, he saw that by each plate was a long spoon. The starving people could not reach their mouth with the spoon and went hungry. In the other room, the people were feeding each other with the spoon.

The power of social entrepreneurs led Bill Drayton to found *Ashoka.* In the past three decades, the global citizen sector (www.ashoka.org/citizensector), led by entrepreneurs, has grown exponentially. Just as the business sector experienced a tremendous spurt in productivity over the last century, the citizen sector is experiencing a similar revolution with the number and sophistication of citizen organizations increasing dramatically. For clarification, "Citizen sector" and "citizen organization" have become words chosen by many non-profit organizations instead of the "non"words. The reason given for this is that when one or several people get together to cause positive social change, they instantly become citizens in the fullest sense of the word.

ABC's World News deserves commendation for airing not only the hard news but also bringing us news that inspires and encourages us to be pro-active in creating a better world. In a broadcast of *PrimeTime Night Time* on ABC, a story headlined, "Saving the American Dream", reported on the efforts of Bruce Boguslav to help people save their homes by fighting the banks for a reduced mortgage and affordable payment. Also, in that broadcast was the story of Purple Heart Homes, founded by Veterans Dale Beatty and John Gallina. Both were severely wounded in Iraq in 2004. Upon learning that a disabled veteran could not get funds to make his home wheel-chair accessible, they stepped in and made the necessary reconstruction. Purple Heart Homes provides, at little or no cost to the veteran, a "quality of life solution" that creates an injury specific, barrier-free-living environment.

In another broadcast, a story was told of a hardware store in Chagrin Falls, Ohio, which was on the brink of closing its doors. The store had opened in 1857 and was purchased by Jack Shutts in 1920. A long- time customer who knew the store was in trouble sent an e-mail asking folks to spend at least $20 on the 21st of the month. The result: 500 customers showed up, and it was the biggest sale day ever. Customers from as far away as San Diego called to order American flags.

Recently, World News with Diane Sawyer aired a program entitled "Made in America". It encouraged families to be aware of the purchases they make, and to buy those products made right here in the United States. In fact, they enlisted the help of one family who agreed to discard everything in their home that was not made in America and replace it with products made in America. That single effort ignited an explosion of people who joined the Made in America movement, and resulted in the creation of thousands of jobs. Made in America continues to be a regular segment on ABC World News. You can join the movement right now by going to www.madeinusa.com and get a list of American made products and where to find them.

# Healthcare and Drugs

The fact that our government has not been able to create a successful health care system speaks for itself. Despite many attempts, our system is flawed in many ways. Health insurance has become unaffordable to many. How can we best assure the health of our citizens? This has been the subject of debate for years. President Obama claims to have the answer. His "Obama care" plan, despite furious opposition, has been put in place. It is still being disputed and the results remain to be seen.

Our bodies are designed to heal themselves. There are those engaged today in holistic healing, and we have seen indisputable proof of what many call "medical miracles". It has been proven that the placebo effect is often just as effective in combatting disease as are drugs. In fact, one-third of medical healing is the result of the placebo effect. Conversely, the nocebo effect (negative thinking) is powerful in keeping us from being healthy.

The drug industry, however, is alive, well and thriving, offering a pharmaceutical solution for nearly every discomfort we might experience. Take a trip to your local drug store and you will see hundreds of prescriptions waiting to be picked up on any given day. Watch the commercials on TV and you will discover there are remedies for ailments you never knew existed. You will hear about drugs for helping you get a good night's sleep, having better sex, relieving body aches so that you can play a better game of golf or frolic with your grandchildren. However, they all come with a list of possible side effects, one of which may be death.

Medicine is controlled by money. It is not in the interest of pharmaceutical companies to support holistic or self- healing. In fact, when a patient seemingly cures himself, medicine simply discounts it. Let me offer my own disclaimer here. I know that there are many life-saving drugs today which have been invaluable in the treatment of disease. There are drugs which contribute in a major way to the quality of life of some individuals. Dr. Elliott Dacher also acknowledges the benefits of medicine in many instances. In 1975, Dr. Dacher began his medical practice in Washington D.C. He served as a practicing internist, physician/administrator and director of wellness and health promotion services for the Kaiser Permanente Health Care Program. In 1984 he established a private practice in Virginia, and began exploring and integrating innovative approaches such as meditation, imagery, yoga, biofeedback and alternative therapies into his day-to-day work with patients. In 1996 he left medical practice to begin an in-depth study of the principles and practices of consciousness and health. This led to his most recent book, *Aware, Awake, Alive* in which he brings together the wisdom and practices of East and West, introducing the reader to a time-tested, practical and accessible approach to far-reaching health and healing. Dr. Dasher reminds us that health is currently only being measured by the wellness of the body, but total wellness and health means human flourishing – stable health and happiness despite circumstances. While we spend money to improve the health of our bodies, we spend far less on maintaining a high quality of life.

Dr. Len Sapulto is another physician with a similar belief. He suggests that lifestyle should be the first step to wellness. He says that our *health* care today is really *disease* care. While Dr. Sapulto recognizes the value of much of our medical breakthroughs today, he has stepped up to advocate for integral medicine. Dr. Saputo is the founder of the Health Medicine Forum, a non-profit educational foundation. Since 1994, "The Forum" has sponsored more than 350 public and professional events including lectures, workshops and conferences. In 2001, Dr. Saputo founded the Health Medicine Center, an integrative medicine center located in Walnut Creek, California. The facility brings the model of Health Medicine into clinical practice. Dr. Saputo believes, as many of our evolutionary leaders do, that we need to BE the change we want to see. Alternative medicine is accepted and being used although not fully integrated into the main stream.

Prayer has also been proven to be an effective healer. Research focusing on the power of prayer has nearly doubled in the last ten years according to David Larson, MD MSPH, president of the National Institute for Healthcare Research, a private non-profit agency. The NIH which, four years ago, refused to review any study which included the word "prayer" is funding one prayer study through its Frontier Medicine Initiative.

My intention in writing this book, as I have stated, is to give you the FACTS and encourage you to research them for yourself. While many of you may agree that the placebo effect is real, here are the facts for those of you who are still skeptical. The world is made up of electro-magnetic energy. Science has shown that, if you change either the electro or magnetic field of an atom, the atom will change. The heart is the strongest electromagnetic generator of the body. Belief happens in the heart. Therefore, if we hold a belief in our heart and can feel the positive outcome, our body responds to those expectations and healing occurs. When we believe we are healed, our brain cells change as if the chemical has worked. Our bodies respond to our expectations when they are created through the heart. I would refer you to Gregg Braden's book, *"Spontaneous Healing of Belief"*.

Remember grandma's old fashioned remedies? Experts have now discovered that white tea, witch hazel and the simple rose have within them many healing properties. In the December 1, 2011 issue of Science Daily, London's Kingston University scientists reported that age-old remedies could hold the key to treating many of our most serious medical problems. They contain properties that have been found to block the progression of inflammation, a vital factor in both the initiation and development of disease. They even keep the skin firmer and less wrinkled.

*Voice for Hope* is an organization striving to advance the wellbeing of humanity. They are working to ensure those offering alternative and integrative health and wellness services and products have meaningful participation in the development of public policy. This would afford the rights of individual consumers and their families to information and access to these products and services. *Creating Action* is the lobbying arm assisting Voice for Hope's mission.

Lori Strolin@voiceforhope.org

# *Education*

One thing that should be indisputable is that the education of our children is one of the most, if not *the* most, important task we have as a nation. Yet we see our schools falling short. Our education system is failing to educate. However, we continue to operate our schools in the same way, teaching the same curriculum and requiring students to learn at the same rate each year until they graduate. While football players and movie stars are drawing millions of dollars in a single month, our teachers are being paid pitifully low salaries. When a state has a budget crisis, education bears the brunt with teachers being laid off. In an article in "Contemporary Issues in Technology and Teacher Education", Thomas Carroll poses the question: "If we didn't have today's schools, would we create today's schools?" He says it is a "trick" question and the trick is that, if we wouldn't create today's schools, what are we doing about it? Carroll says if we continue to prepare teachers as we have always prepared them, we are going to continue to recreate the schools we have always had. Remember the definition of insanity? It is doing the same thing over and over and expecting different results. Carroll goes on to ask if a surgeon from the 1880's walked into an operating room today where arthroscopic surgery was being performed, could he step in and perform that surgery? Probably not. If a teacher from the 1800's walked into a classroom today, could he or she substitute as a teacher? There would obviously be new technology with the computers, but would the basic instruction be the same? Perhaps it's time to take a look at our educational system and determine whether it is meeting the needs of today's learners.

Salman Khan has done just that. On a recent segment of Sixty Minutes, we were introduced to the Khan Academy founded by Salman Khan and supported by Bill Gates and Google. The concept is free education for every human being on planet Earth. Sound crazy? I invite you to visit the website at www.khanacademy.org and learn about this innovative program for yourself.

There are "alternative" schools privately run in this country, and many parents elect to home school their children. However, federally funded mainstream schools remain the major source of education for our youth today. These children will become the leaders of the next century. It is our responsibility to adequately prepare them for that role.

# *Security*

One of our Government's mandates is to keep us safe. In keeping with that mandate, the Army, Navy and Marine Corps were established in 1776 in concurrence with the American Revolution. That led to the establishment of the War Department in 1789. The War Department was originally responsible for the operation and maintenance of the United States Army, and for Naval affairs until the establishment of the Navy Department in 1798, and for most land-based air forces until the creation of the Department of the Air Force in 1947. Ultimately in 1949, all military branches were consolidated and placed under what is now known as the Department of Defense. Many people believe that we have a warrior instinct, and that our nature is to fight. Some believe that war is as natural as night and day, something that all humans do. I understand that the wars that were fought many years ago may have been necessary to give us the freedoms we enjoy today. World War I, declared by President Woodrow Wilson in 1917, was fought on the premise that America's aid was essential in securing civilization. The Second World War was entered into on December 8,1941 in retaliation to the attack on Pearl Harbor. However, according to Norman Soloman, author of *War Made Easy*, civilians accounted for fifteen percent of the casualties in World War I, 65 percent in World War II and more than 90 percent of the casualties in Iraq. According to many historians, the death toll for World War II stands at about 50 million human lives! We mourn the loss of these lives and those of our young soldiers who lost their lives and call it "collateral damage". Each of these persons was created and put here on earth for a purpose. What might they have done had their lives not been snuffed out by gunfire? Each life that is lost in war affects more than just one person. There are children who will grow up without a father or mother, wives and husbands who will never have the opportunity to grow old together, and families torn apart. War is shameful and we can do better.

Wars in the past have been fought over borders and boundaries. The beginning and end of the war were clearly defined. There was an unmistakable winner. How do we fight a war over how someone believes? We have labeled those who want to attack us because we do not believe as they do terrorists. Certainly their actions have created terror. And I understand our need to do what we deem necessary to save our lives and those of our loved ones and fellow citizens. However, when faced with a threat to our security, whether real or perceived, our first reaction is often to prepare to retaliate and kill. If there is only the suspicion of an impending threat, the discussion revolves around how we might attack. Do we use air power or boots on the ground?

We are, by nature, a peaceful people. When we deviate from that nature, it is due to a threat on our personal safety, that of our families or to our way of life. Fear keeps us stuck in our old paradigm and prevents us from exploring new and more peaceful means of settling conflicts. When we feel threatened in any way or another country asks for our help, our first response is to fight. That leads to a build-up of our military and a monetary outlay. When we do engage in "war", we lose many of the most precious resources we have on this planet, our young men and women. How might those dollars have been spent if not for our so-called "defense"?

People have been demonstrating against war for many years. They don't have a real solution, but they believe strongly that war is not the answer to anything. The Peace Alliance was formed to create a culture of peace on our planet. Their goal is to have our Government create a U.S. Department of Peace. Their demonstrations are peaceful and their mantra is to be *for peace* rather than *against war.* Their focus is to lobby our legislators to create this legislation. That has proven to be a daunting task, but the effort continues. How logical would it be it that what was once the War Department and then became the Department of Defense would now become the Department of Peace?

The Department of Peace would research peaceful ways of resolving conflict. There would be a Peace Academy where young men and women would learn the art of peacemaking. They would study the cultures of other countries to better understand and communicate with them in times of conflict. They would work WITH the military to assist in easing tensions and creating trust among the people in conflict. Omar Nelson Bradley was a senior United States army field commander in North Africa and Europe during World War II and a general of the army in the United States. He is credited with a number of quotes, two of which I want to share with you:

> *"Ours is a world of nuclear giants and ethical infants. We know more about war than we know about peace, more about killing than we know about living." "Wars can be prevented just as surely as they can be provoked; and we who fail to prevent them must share the guilt for the dead."*

War has become a way of life on this planet. But it was not always the case. Wars actually began to occur just 5000 years ago, the last age of the Mayan Calendar. This is the age we are in now. Our ancestors predicted that this 5000 year cycle would be dark. We have seen this exhibited in numerous wars, violence, and abuse of one another. However, they also predicted that this next cycle would be one of peace. This, of course, is predicated on whether or not we make it through our present cycle.

Another organization, Beyond War (www.beyondwar.org) is a non-political educational organization that has been working since 1984 to support a growing movement to change planetary thinking about war. Beyond War invites people to become everyday peace-builders everywhere and to truly live beyond war. Their mission is to explore model and promote the means for humanity to live beyond war.

Conflict and war do not occur just between countries. We see violence on our streets and gang wars. There is violence in our homes and in our schools on a daily basis. Bullying is running rampant. The Department of Peace would address violence at home with courses taught in the early school years which show children how to resolve their differences in a peaceful manner and how to respect one another regardless of their differences.

Violence and crime are motivated by the fear of not having enough to survive. Those in lack feel they must fight for what they need and take from others if necessary. When we can dispel the belief that, if you have more I have less or none, we will all experience abundance and plenty. War is based on the same thing. We want to protect our land and our freedom from those we believe would take it from us.

Despite the violence, crime and corruption that are prevalent in our society today, we are altruistic beings at our core. Our basic instinct is to help people. Whenever a disaster occurs anywhere in the world, people come together to offer aid in the form of money, food, clothing, and medical assistance. There are thousands of organizations committed to helping alleviate hunger, homelessness, drug addiction, domestic violence and much other blight on our civilization. Every day we hear about people who have risked their own lives to save the life of someone whose life is being threatened. They didn't stop to think about it. Many times they did not even know the individual. They acted on impulse which comes from our true nature to help one another

We can take care of one another. Organizations have been created to be of service to others in need. Communities have organizations to feed the hungry, provide shelter for the homeless, and safety and security for those in harm's way from their own family. Faith based organizations help their congregants. If we became a world where taking care of our "brothers and sisters" was a high priority and even expected of us, we could reduce the cost of government programs that have skyrocketed our national debt to trillions.

The Centers for Disease Control and Prevention has funded UNITY (Urban Networks to Increase Thriving Youth) as part of the CDC's national youth violence prevention initiative, STRYVE (Striving to Reduce Youth Violence Everywhere). Learn more at www.preventioninstitute.org

Conflict is inevitable. There will always be disagreement between individuals, families and, of course nations. The key here is to resolve the conflict before it escalates into violence or war. Most often, when conflict does arise, it is a "right fight". One party is adamant about being right and willing to go to any lengths to 'win" the battle. Therefore, the key to resolving the conflict peacefully is overlooked. That key is distinguishing between the real problem and the special interest of the parties involved. Search for Common Ground, (SFCG) is an organization founded by John Marks over 20 years ago. Their mission is "Understand the differences; act on the commonalities".

There are techniques for resolving conflicts and for communicating in a non-violent manner. I refer you to Marshall Rosenberg, founder and developer of Nonviolent Communication (NVC) The Conflict Resolution Network is a source for training materials and support for educators to learn tools and strategies for resolving conflicts in a peaceful manner.

# *Change*

Change is constant. Our bodies, our Universe, and all livng things are constantly changing. We may not be able to see some of these changes, but they are occurring. Many of the changes we **can** see. They are happening faster and faster as the pace of our lives speeds up. An obvious example is technology. Most of the technology today was science fiction just a few short years ago. Technology, science and inventions have progressed at an accelerated rate during the hundred years of the 20th century more than any other century. We began the 20th century with airplanes, automobiles and radio, and those inventions dazzled us with their novelty and wonder. We end the 20th century with spaceships, cellphones and the wireless internet. Who would have thought that something you can hold in the palm of your hand would be capable of paying bills, taking pictures and accessing information from the internet? The internet, itself, is an amazing phenomenon. Type a few words on a keyboard and access information in seconds. Remember the old encyclopedias? Now, instead perusing through pages of information, we can just "google it". Today we can send messages and pictures to thousands of people around the world with one click of a button. Remember letters? Snail Mail as it is now called is still around, but click and send is faster. The advancements continue to increase at shorter and shorter intervals. Changes are literally occurring by the minute. Purchase a television, computer, or cell phone and, within months, there is new technology which makes your purchase almost obsolete. Calculations that would have taken decades in the past are now are made in minutes. Communication has gone from days to seconds.

There is a reason for this. Each new development builds on the current one, so much of the work has already been done. All that is needed is the "upgrade" or the technology to make it better. Where did the ideas for the improvements come from? They came from YOU, the inventor. They began with YOU thinking about how that device or procedure could be better, faster, more accurate, easier to operate, etc. etc. If we can effect changes in technology with our thoughts and ideas, why can't we use our thoughts to impact the thinking and attitudes of the people of the earth towards a more peaceful and sustainable way of living? We can! We begin by being aware of our own attitudes and beliefs and recognizing when they may need to be changed.

Thanks to the internet, shopping, paying bills, banking and many other daily activities have been made easier and faster. If we chose to, we would rarely have to leave home. Microwaves have changed the way we cook and eat. While many of these changes have made our lives easier, they have also contributed to our faster pace of living. We love convenience and we want it now! Hungry? Choose a fast food restaurant, drive through, order and pick up your food in minutes.

Our demand for instant gratification has its downside. Discarded plastic bags and styrofoam containers are a major contributor to pollution. When we enjoy a nice meal at a restaurant, we ask for a "doggy bag". This used to be for the bones and leftover or fatty meat that was actually meant for our dog. Today, we ask for a container in which to take our "left-overs". My thought is why not bring a Tupperware or other re-usable container from your kitchen if you expect to take leftovers home from an evening of dining out? Perhaps an even better solution is for restaurants to serve smaller portions or at least offer a selection of portion size. Grocery stores are now encouraging the use of reusable bags and many shoppers have responded to this.

If changes in technology have made our lives easier and more convenient, what might be the result of changes in our way of governing, educating, providing healthcare, doing business and maintaining a peaceful and secure planet? Who will make these changes and how will they come about? They will be made by the Evolutionary Leaders, the Cultural Creatives, and the Imaginal cells. They will be made by you and by me working together with others to bring about the changes needed for our planet and our civilization to survive and thrive.

Changes in technology have paved the way for us to become a global family. We are connected to each and every living thing on this planet and possibly the entire Universe. The Internet, cell phones, I-phones and other devices which allow us to communicate with our friends and send pictures and videos are a visible demonstration of this connection. The power of this connection, I believe, has yet to be seen. It is imperative that we recognize this and use it responsibly. People working together for positive change and making their voices heard can change the course of history. I remind you again of Margaret Mead's statement: "Never doubt that a small group of thoughtful committed citizens can change the world. Indeed it is the only thing that ever has."

Change! It is such a small word with such enormous impact. Substitute the word "evolution" for change. This is a time when we can create a new paradigm for living on this planet. Dr. Lipton suggests that this evolution will result in a super organism called Humanity. Barbara Marx Hubbard calls it "Birth 2012". I call it waking up to who we really are…beings of Love.

# *My Vision for Our Future*

**Energy/Environment**

Cultural creatives with great minds will create an alternative to fossil fuels. Although this has already been done, it will be accepted and implemented so that we are not dependent on oil as the main source of our energy needs. Automobiles will be manufactured which are fueled by substances other than oil. Because we now recognize ourselves as a planetary community, we will share our resources so that all countries will have an abundant supply of whatever they need to maintain a high quality of life. We will see our planet as a living entity and respect it by keeping it clean and free of pollution. We will respect the habitats of our fellow creatures that live in the forests, the oceans and deserts. We will learn how to share our space here on this planet so we can all live in a healthy environment. We will cherish and respect the energy in our bodies, recognizing that thoughts use energy and always strive for balance in growth and protection. We will understand the energy of money, use it wisely and share it generously.

## Government

How might an "imagineer" or "cultural creative" change our system of Government? It seems obvious to me that the two party system is not working. Because the Republicans and Democrats are so entrenched in their own ideology, they are unwilling or unable to look at another point of view. As a result, what may be the best solution falls by the wayside. I would dissolve the labels of republican, democrat, independent, libertarian and any others. Those interested in serving our country as president or their state as senator or representative would announce their candidacy. Several round table discussions or debates would be held at which each candidate would put forth his or her vision for what they would bring to the office. There would be no radio or television ads. Candidates could use the social media which is available to everyone to enlist support. The primary election would narrow the field of candidates down to two or possibly three top vote getters depending on how close the votes were in the primary election. The president would be elected by a vote of all of the people and the senators and representatives by a vote of the people in their state or district. Remember, there would be no democrats, republicans, independents or libertarians. They would just be candidates for office.

Men and women who have and are running for office have a great deal of money. Many are millionaires. As they begin their campaigns, their coffers are then stuffed with more money from special interest groups and corporations. That money is used to buy advertising. The result: the candidate with the most money and most creative (or destructive) advertising wins!! That is the reason I would propose to disallow paid advertising . Social media and networking is available and affordable for everyone. With the use of Face Book, Twitter, Tweets and e-mail, I believe that candidates would be able to easily get their message across to the millions of people they want to reach.

Even with major changes such as the dissolution of political parties, there will be differences of opinion in Congress as they engage in the process of lawmaking. Those differences could be more easily reconciled if each of our elected lawmakers comes to the office with certification of training in nonviolent communication and conflict management. If there comes a time when there seems to be a stalemate, however, it will be resolved by mandatory arbitration. That person could either be the speaker of the house, fully accredited in mediation techniques, or a hired mediator from outside. Today our candidates are touting their experience in business and money management. After all, it's the economy s....d. How about skills in peacebuilding, ethical business practices or environmental management? Our senators and representatives would encourage suggestions from their constituents in all areas and give them full consideration. This could easily be done on Facebook. There is a wealth of great ideas hidden in the grass roots.

## Economic/Finance

This is an area in which, I will admit, I do not have a great deal of expertise or knowledge. However, I do know that the recent financial crisis which we experienced was caused by greed and corruption. Mom and pop stores have been pushed out by the big box stores and giant corporations. Bruce Lipton, in his book *Spontaneous Evolution* gives an analogy of corporations to dinosaurs. In his chapter on "Fractal Evolution", pages 238-239, he tells us that the word *dinosaur* is a Greek word meaning "terrifying monstrous lizard." Bruce goes on to say that as dinosaurs' bodies became enlarged, their brains remained small. In comparing the dinosaur to corporations, he suggests that corporations have large bodies of administrative bureaucracies commanded by decision-making executives with small, reptilian brains. The dinosaurs became extinct due to the fact that their under-sized brain, although able to support amazing reflex behaviors, wasn't adequate to sustain survival of their massive bodies during times of environmental upheaval. The so-called brains of conventional corporations are effective when controlling the reflexive behavior and growth of their organizations as long as the environment stays stable. They lack the neurological ability to control and adapt their massive bodies to survive in environments that are in upheaval. Stockholders in large corporations expect a generous return on their investment. What if there were no stockholders? What if a corporation's success was based on how much they contributed to the community to enhance the quality of life. Since 1946, Target has donated five percent of its profits to local community outreach and is on track to reach one billion dollars by the end of 2015.

## Health

We are far too dependent on drugs for our health. That being said, I know that drugs have saved millions of lives and have served to eradicate many fatal diseases such as measles, whooping cough, diphtheria, polio and others. I also know that drugs have enabled persons with diabetes and other diseases to lead a much more comfortable and enjoyable life. In the future, we would see alternative medicine come to the fore as a way of preventing these diseases. These practitioners would work side by side with physicians and other medical professionals to provide the best health care. Prayer would always be an option to be incorporated with any medical treatment. Children, during their yearly checkup, would be schooled, age appropriately, on nutrition and other ways to create and maintain a healthy lifestyle. They would learn to respect their bodies and make food and lifestyle choices accordingly. The key word here is "choice". I would never advocate for mandating how we must live our lives. However, when our children grow up learning how to maintain a healthy lifestyle, it would follow that they would ultimately become healthy adults.

## Education

How would an "imagineer" design our schools? Perhaps we might go back to the one room schoolhouse. Many years ago, there were only a few children in each grade so they were all in one room with one teacher. While the one room schoolhouse may not work going forward today, the concept might. What if subjects were taught to groups of students at the appropriate "learning level" instead of at their grade level? Rooms that were formerly designated for each grade level would be assigned by subject. In addition to the traditional studies such as math, reading, social studies, etc. students would have the opportunity to choose one or two elective subjects such as cooking, nutrition, astrology, architecture, braille, and a wealth of others. Teachers would be alert to the special talents or knowledge exhibited by their students and guide them to develop it. Art and music would be available to all students beginning in grade one. The result: adults who are skilled in what they truly love and are able to make a living for themselves and a valuable contribution to society.

## Security

The word security has many meanings. Perhaps the most widely held is safety. One of the mandates of our government is to keep us safe. How would an imagineer see the role of ensuring the safety and security of the people here on planet Earth? First, we would see ourselves as one world family. Holding that belief, we would be less inclined to see the actions of others on the planet as threats to our safety. We would hold out our hands and hearts to our neighbors instead of stockpiling weapons "just in case". Second, we would, of course, be awake and aware. If we perceive danger to ourselves or to our neighbors, we would be swift to act. We would be aware of the needs of others and do whatever we could to assist them. With regard to our national security, the Department of Peace (which will have been established) would respond to perceived threats in a non-violent peaceful manner. I truly believe that the so-called "terrorists" are simply human beings with an erroneous belief. Just as we have held many beliefs that we now know to be false, these fellow human citizens can be shown that their beliefs are false, and that they can live in peace with others who do not share their ideology. I am not naïve enough to believe that this will happen quickly or without turmoil, but I am confident that it *can* happen.

41

In 2005, an issue of Scientific American featured an article entitled, "Crossroads for Planet Earth" which focused on the challenges of the next fifty years and how our choices may well determine our species ability not only to thrive but to survive far into the future. This drew numerous letters from readers offering criticisms, answers and even prognostications. The warning in this issue was not doom and gloom, and was capsulized by a quote from Apple computer visionary, Alan C Kay: "The best way to predict the future is to invent it. Fortunately, we are all "inventors" if we choose to be.

# *Awareness*

In order to bring about change, we need to be aware that change is needed. Just what does that mean? It means being awake. Look at the world we have created thus far. As Dr. Phil would say, "How's it workin' for you?" Are you enjoying a healthy quality of life? Do you experience joy and love in your daily life? Do you feel safe and secure? Do you have what you need to maintain a healthy prosperous life, one in which you are able to contribute to the wellbeing of planet Earth and its inhabitants? Are there things you see that disturb you? Does life seem to be a constant struggle?

Most of us are aware of the obvious things that are deplorable on our planet today. Our young men and women are dying in foreign lands "to keep us safe and free". Children are killing each other in our schools and on the street. Our neighbors are sleeping on the streets and ravaging through trash cans for food. When I hear that one out of six persons in this country, the United States of America, goes hungry, it seems unbelievable. Many people cannot find employment and are losing their homes. Others are bringing in salaries in the millions of dollars. I am not implying that those people do not deserve their wealth and good fortune. But, in a country which proclaims to be a world leader and offers unlimited opportunity, choice and freedom, do poverty and homelessness have a place? When disaster strikes such as a tsunami or major earthquake, we instinctively run to help others across the street or across the globe with food, money and clothing. Yet often we walk right by our neighbor sleeping on the street. Do we not consider the plight of that neighbor a catastrophe worthy of our aid?

As people begin to wake up and become aware that a change is needed, they often gravitate to what most disturbs them and become active in advocating for change. Demonstrations and marches against war have been going on for some time. Today we see people gathered together to "occupy Wall Street". This was triggered by the meltdown and corruption in our financial and real estate systems. While these folks don't have an answer or solution, they know that a change needs to be made. Unfortunately, some of their activities caused the police to intervene and both sides experienced violence. However, they are being heard.

Groups and organizations have formed to address specific causes or issues particularly around the environment, conflict and war and health. Many people, who I consider Visionaries, have been studying these changes and their meaning for many years. Through the Internet, they have found a way to educate others and inspire action. When I began receiving e-mails from groups like Evolutionary Leaders, The Conscious Activist, The Aware Show, The Shift Network, Beyond Awakening and others and listening to dozens of hour long tele-seminars, their messages resonated with me. These were beliefs and ideas I have held for years. They are what prompted me to write this book and share their message with as many people as possible. I have included information on many of these groups at the end of this book.

# *We Are Connected*

The Internet is a perfect example of what science has known since the creation of the Universe. We are all connected! Because we could not actually see this connection, we came to believe in separation. We looked at ourselves and others as individual entities. We considered ourselves separate and sometimes superior to others who differed from us in skin color, ethnicity, religious practices and even occupations and geographical locations. The internet and social media have shown us our connection in ways never before dreamed. Satellites enable us to watch from our living rooms as an event takes place across the globe. The Internet has proven to be an incredible tool for getting information to large groups of people. We can have face to face communication with thousands of people at one time. We can take pictures of an event as it is happening and send them off to someone across the globe in seconds. We connect with one another via cell phones, on facebook, twitter and other social media. Not only do we talk to one another on our cell phone, we can text them. And many young folks are doing it twenty-four-seven. It has become so widespread that laws have been enacted prohibiting people from talking or texting while driving an automobile. This led to the development of "hands free" technology so that we could continue to be connected even while driving. Everywhere I go, I see people talking or texting as they push a baby stroller, walk a dog, walk down the street or even sit on the beach. In fact, texting has led to the development of a whole new language. Facebook allows a group of people to communicate among themselves and learn firsthand what their friends and their friend's friends are doing on a daily basis. When someone posts a comment, it can be read and responded to by literally hundreds, even thousands of people who are "friends" with the writer. In addition to social use, businesses use this social networking as a way to promote their business.

What do we do, however, when we become "disconnected". When our batteries in our cell phone die or when the power goes out on our computer, we are lost. We have always had a connection with our source and with every other being in the Universe. The connection is through our hearts, and there are no batteries or internet connection needed. When we feel stressed or fearful, angry or isolated, we have become temporarily disconnected from our Source. This is the time to take a moment and "reconnect". This can be done through meditation. It can also be done using tools created by HeartMath, which is discussed later in the book.

When civilization began, it was easy to see our connection. The first people living on this earth lived in close-knit clans. They could never have imagined the sprawling cities and travel by air as a way of life. Even just a few hundred years ago, families lived together, often two or three generations in one household. Children grew up and remained in the same town, sometimes even the same home. They worked and raised their families there. Often children remained in the same home after their parents were deceased. When communities evolved into large cities and transportation became easier, children left home to attend a college, raise a family or work at a job outside their hometown. They became disconnected from the close knit family structure of the past. The need to belong and to connect remains an innate part of each of us. We join a fraternity or sorority, we belong to a gang, or we become a member of the Lions Club, Kiwanis, PTA or other social organization. Health care professionals have learned that those suffering from heart disease and other illnesses are more likely to live an isolated life without social connections.

We have become a global society whether we like it or not. Technology has put us in close touch with every person on the planet. Just as the North and South had to come together to create our great nation, so too, must the countries of the world come together to create a sustainable planet and a world that works for everyone. I have always been of the belief that we are spiritual beings of Love, and that it is possible to live in peace with everyone and everything on our planet. I also believe that we live in an abundant Universe, and that there need never be even one person that does not have enough food, money or shelter.

# *Cooperation Versus Competition*

One of the most crucial changes that must happen is the change from a culture of competition to one of cooperation. This means that we need to change our belief in *survival of the fittest*. This will undoubtedly be a daunting challenge as our society is based on competition to achieve success. Charles Darwin, in trying to explain human existence, based some of his thinking on his observance of the animal kingdom. He noticed that when two birds of the same kind were in a nest and another bird which was different approached that nest, the birds rejected it. He also observed that a colony of large ants captured colonies of smaller ants and made them do the work. His law then, (back in 1859) implied that humans were to *multiply, vary and let the strongest live and the weakest die.* Can you see how that thinking has manifested in some of our behavior today? We have justified this survival of the strongest thinking by pointing to the animal kingdom and the "food chain". However, studies have shown that animals demonstrate more cooperation than competition. In his book, *Mutual Aid: A Factor of Evolution*, Petr Alekseevich Kropotkin asserted that natural selection favors cooperation, not competition. Kropotkin suggested that the struggle for existence is due more to environmental causes such as extreme heat or cold, and that animals join forces in these kinds of struggles. Animals can also warn other animals of impending attack.

I remind you that my intention in writing this book is to bring you the facts. There have been 400 studies done to determine what the ideal amount of competition is in *any* environment: business, politics, space, sports, education or any other field. The results of that study showed that the optimum amount of competition is **zero!** Competition is always destructive.

A leading critic of competition is Alfie Kohn. In his book *No Contest: The Case Against Competition*, he discusses the destructive effects of win/lose arrangements at school, at home, at play and also at work. He showed how competitiveness and excellence tend to pull in opposite directions regardless of whether in a classroom, office or entire society. A subsequent book, *Punished by Rewards: the Trouble with Gold Stars, Incentive Plans, A's Praise and other Bribes* became required reading in business schools and corporations, and has attracted the attention of teachers, parents and psychologists.

Businesses compete with one another for customers. They strive to become number one! Kohn believes that the more an individual or organization is focused on being Number One, the less likely that quality can be maintained. Since being number one usually means being the one with the largest profit, that assumption seems accurate. In order to gain more profit, cheap labor is used by outsourcing to other countries. Mom and pop businesses could not possibly compete with the Big Box companies resulting in many having to close their doors. Salespersons within a company compete to be the top producer. Of course, that means the salesperson that brings in the most dollars. Did the salesperson need to stretch the truth or somehow persuade the customer to buy just to close the sale? If the bottom line is simply money, where does that leave service and integrity?

Our focus on competition and equating success with money has led to our economic downfall in a big way. Can we look at how we do business with "new eyes" and envision a way that will be good for the economy, the consumer *and* the business? It is not only possible, it is essential! I again refer to Albert Einstein who has said that problems cannot be solved with the same mind that created them. In other words, we cannot solve a problem by remaining in our current state of consciousness. That means that the solution must be based on a whole new way of thinking.

Although it may be one of our greatest challenges, we can, I believe, change from a competition based mentality to one of cooperation. If you are shaking your head and saying sports is the exception, I invite you to hold that thought. Many of the youth sports organizations have opted not to "keep score" as these young boys and girls begin to learn the game of basketball, football, soccer and baseball.

With regard to the competition in our national sports, consider this: After a major victory by some sports teams, celebrations have turned into riots and mass destruction of property. There have been reports of football players being paid to deliberately injure a player on a competing team. While these may be isolated incidents and not the norm, I leave you with the challenge to simply explore the alternatives to winning and losing.

Earlier I talked about technology and the fact that improvements and new discoveries in technology are occurring at shorter and shorter intervals. The reason for this is that each new innovation is built on the knowledge that preceded it. As this continues, we will see an upward spiral as new and almost unbelievable technology is created. The United States has been in competition with Russia in the area of space exploration. If we shared our information and technology, new discoveries and innovations might result in less time. Working together with other countries, discoveries might be made that would not only be of value in our space expeditions, but might spill over into the areas of health, environmental and other areas. We could also end world hunger by cooperating and sharing our resources. In addition, by working together, we would have no reason to fear that some country might have technology that could harm us either physically or financially. The barrier to achieving this kind of cooperation is fear. We have been living in a fear based society for hundreds of years, and it will likely take some time to begin to believe we can actually live in peace with our "perceived" enemies. The operating premise here would be trust. We would need to develop trust among the nations with whom we cooperate. This may not be easy, but it *is* possible.

# *Cultural Creatives*

When British historian Arnold Toynbee introduced the notion that the cultural mainstream clings to fixed ideas and rigid patterns even in the face of imposing environmental challenges, he also maintained that threatening challenges would inevitably be resolved by what he described as creative minorities, known today as Cultural Creatives. These people transform old, outdated philosophical truths into new, life sustaining cultural beliefs. There are many organizations out there today doing just that. They are called Evolutionary Leaders and Conscious Evolutionists. Bruce Lipton calls them, in comparing the cells in our body to human beings on our planet, *Imaginal* cells. These individuals understand where our evolution must take us if we are to survive and create a world free of hatred, violence, poverty, war and scarcity. They are the visionaries for the future not unlike the prophets of long ago. There is one monumental difference, however. You and I can become one of them. If you are open to these new ideas and the evidence science has uncovered and, if you are willing to learn more, you can be one of the evolutionary leaders, a cultural creative, an *imaginal* cell. I have listed many of these organizations and individuals in my reference section. When we evolve into this super organism that Dr. Lipton calls humanity, we will understand that not only is it our responsibility to take care of ourselves, but it is also our responsibility to help others. We will not rush to blame someone else when a disaster occurs, but begin to find ways to be of service in rectifying the problem or finding a solution.

Early in 2011, we saw the people of Egypt rise up and overthrow a government that no longer worked for them. Then Lybia followed their example. What is motivating these young people to suddenly rise up from years of tyranny and oppression and demand their freedom? Could a change in the earth's magnetic field be a factor? People are experiencing a shift in consciousness which manifests in taking action to be free of oppression and violence. They are realizing they deserve to live in freedom from tyranny and have the power to do so. The Mayan prophecies, which tell of the end of a 5125 year cycle and beginning of the next, indicate that this next cycle will be one of conscious evolution for humanity. They predict that in this next 5125 year cycle, we will see humanity become more loving and compassionate. We will experience a peaceful era without war and we will begin to heal our planet.

Bruce Lipton, in his book *Spontaneous Evolution*, talks about biological imperatives, those drives within us for basic needs of food, shelter, water, etc. He says that when those needs are threatened, we have an early warning mechanism which shifts into play and we begin to take action. There are those among us who recognize that something is not right, and many of our current systems are not working. They have no solutions and do not know what to do. By demonstrating and protesting, people are responding to what they perceive as a threat to their survival.

Our way of life as we know it has been the only way we have ever known with few exceptions. So what do we do? Where do we start? We need to begin with an open mind. First of all, just suppose that this shift on our planet **is** occurring and that it does affect us psychologically and emotionally. Second, presume that the demonstrations we are seeing with regard to Wall Street and political unrest around the globe **are** triggered by a threat to our biological imperatives. What kind of changes might we envision with regard to our health system, our political system, our economic and monetary system, our environment and energy?

Referring to Bruce Lipton once again, Bruce says that demonstrations like "Occupy Wall Street" will lead to "emergence". When individuals are brought together, something new can emerge. In comparing it to our body, Bruce says that just one cell could never conceive of going to the moon; however, when trillions of cells come together to create a human body, many things are possible including going to the moon. And when billions of cells (humans) come together as one, the possibilities are mind-blowing and endless.

By going deeper into the study of cells, Dr. Lipton concluded that an individual cell and a human body share similar functions and needs in their quest to survive. His question was: if 50 trillion cells can live in harmony and peace in the human body, why are 7 billion people on planet earth unable to live in peace with each other? In the beginning, life consisted of single cell organisms such as bacteria, algae and amoeba-like protozoans. When they reached their capacity to evolve further, they organized into communities, and multicellular organisms (plants and animals) appeared. Through evolution these cells organized into more communities of trillions of cells. In order to survive, the cells created structured environments and sub-divided the workload. Individual cells formed a community with each one responsible for a specific function. When all of the cells are doing their job and working together, we have a healthy body.

In early civilizations when families lived together, their main priority was survival. Each member worked to find food, shelter and keep themselves safe from harm. As communities began to evolve, individuals took on specific tasks just as the cells did. When people band together in communities and work together to create a healthy, happy environment, all members thrive. When a member (cell) deviates from its job or fails to perform, the entire community (body) suffers. So we can see how deviant or selfish behavior of a few individuals can create dissonance in a community or a planet. When all of the cells (humans) in a family, community, nation or world come together in a unified purpose, the result would have to be a world without war, hunger or hate; a world of love, peace and prosperity for all.

# *The Shift*

The end of another 5125 year cycle and the beginning of the next is not really significant. What is significant is that more and more people are becoming aware of what is not working on our planet and taking action to change it. Others contend that our world is "going to hell in a hand basket" and there is nothing we can do about it. Some fundamentalists see this as the coming of the end of the world when only the faithful believers in Jesus Christ will survive. Many others just plod along in their life oblivious to anything but what is right in front of them.

Many spiritual teachers refer to what is happening as a "shift". As our planet shifts, so does our consciousness. We may begin to think differently about our way of life or often experience feelings we can't explain. We simply know something is stirring within us. Many have acted on those feelings by stepping up and speaking out about the damage we are doing to our environment. Others have been pro-active in an effort to end violence within families and against children. We are seeing the increased activity of ordinary (or should I say extraordinary) citizens and citizen sector (aka non-profit) organizations becoming active in addressing problems such as poverty, war, violence, terrorism and environmental pollution, areas in which the government has proven to be less than effective. Paul Hawkins, in his book *Blessed Unrest*, has documented a million or more of these groups worldwide. If you do a Google search you will find hundreds of thousands of Cultural Creatives, each stepping up in an effort to make the changes needed for our survival. In 2010, Dr. Wayne Dyer, internationally renowned author and speaker, wrote the book *The Shift: Taking Your Life from Ambition to Meaning*. It was a companion book to the movie of the same name.

The Shift Network was launched in February 2010 with Stephen Dinan as CEO. Its aim is to empower a global movement of people who are creating an evolutionary shift of consciousness that will lead to a more enlightened society, one built on principles of sustainability, peace, health and prosperity. I have included more on the Shift Network in my resource section.

The year 2012 represents a great cosmic choice point. Jean Houston calls this period "jump time". She defines it as the changing of the guard on every level in which every "given" is quite literally up for grabs. It shakes the foundation of all and everything, and allows for another order of reality to come into time. This coincides with Gregg Braden's view that, during this period, those systems that are sustainable will prevail and those that are not will collapse.

In an essay by Karl Maret, MD, author of *Awakening the Dialogue of the Heart,* he explores several cosmic events and cycles related to 2012. It is anticipated that, during the remaining years of the Piscean Age, humanity will see some of the greatest breakthroughs in scientific discoveries, technological advancement and health-care achievements, all of which may lead to a cultural renaissance and the possible emergence of a *Universal Humanity*. Dr. Maret also predicts that, during the remaining years of the Piscean age, we on planet Earth will rediscover the importance of engaging our "heart energies" in creating a peaceful and sustainable planet. Later, I will discuss Heart Math and the work of Howard Martin and others in this field.

# *Matters of the Heart*

Love is a four letter word. Love has many meanings. Nearly all religions teach that we must love God and love our neighbor as we love ourselves. But do we practice that kind of love or just give it lip service? If we are to love ourselves and others, where does that love come from? It comes from our heart. And we all have a heart.

Studies now show that changes in the earth's magnetic field are associated with changes in the brain and nervous system activity. Changes in geomagnetic conditions affect the rhythms of the heart more strongly than all the physiological functions studied so far. This can be measured. We have the ability to create powerful emotion in our hearts, and that can affect the magnetic field of the earth.

The heart does more than pump blood. It actually has a nervous system (a brain in the heart). It has been proven that the heart sends more to the brain than the brain sends to the heart. The heart produces oxytocin, a love hormone. As an electrical organ, the heart creates an electro-magnetic field beyond the body. Thus we actually broadcast our feelings. Most of us have experienced this. When we walk into a room or are among a group of people, we can actually *feel* the energy whether it's positive or negative.

Our brain is a thinking tool, but science has now shown us that the heart is much smarter than the brain. In fact, the electromagnetic system of the heart is five thousand times stronger than the brain's electromagnetic field. That means that heart based decisions are generally much better than those thought out by our brains. Studies have confirmed that when we have a thought, that thought is first sent to the heart. The heart, based on the emotion of the thought, then sends a signal to the brain as to how to behave. For a scientific explanation of this, please refer to *Spontaneous Evolution* by Bruce Lipton. In my opinion, that means that trusting our hearts in making decisions will often result in a better outcome than trusting our heads. When we really look at what the heart does in our body, can we discount its power?

Founded by Doc Childre, the **Institute of Heart Math** has as its mission *to help establish heart based living and global coherence by inspiring people to connect with the intelligence and guidance of their heart.* Heart Math is a system, one minute techniques, to connect with intelligence of the heart and reach a higher level of thinking. Heart is the new intelligence. It is reached by the flow of awareness that we experience once the mind and bodily emotions are brought into balance, resulting in coherence.

The Institute of Heart Math actually has technology which can change your heart rhythm pattern to create coherence, a scientifically measurable state characterized by increased order and harmony in our psychological and physiological processes. It collects pulse data through a pulse center and translates the information from your heart rhythms into graphics on your computer or into easy to follow lights on the portable *emwave* personal stress reliever. The result is that anger, anxiety or frustration can be replaced by clarity, ease and peace.

Heart Math has made this technology available to schools and health care facilities as well as the military. It has been proven effective in reducing stress, calming anger and reducing bullying. It has also been effective in treating disease and many traumatic stress disorders. You will find information on the Institute of Heart Math and related organizations in the reference section. By now, it should be clear; we are all connected and able to live in harmony with one another and with our bodies if we choose to do so.

**The Global Coherence Initiative** is a collaborative research project with the Institute of Heart Math, Dr. Elizabeth Rauscher and other engineers to design, build and maintain a Global Coherence Monitoring System. (GCMS) The Global Coherence Monitoring System will establish a worldwide network of sensing stations to measure fluctuations in the earth's geomagnetic fields. These sensors send out a signal every thirty minutes which show the strengths of the magnetic fields of the earth. This is important because we now know that we are connected to those fields. The rhythm of these fields has a natural ebb and flow. However, on September 11, 2001, the rhythm spiked to an unprecedented level. This was caused by human heart based emotion such as anger, fear and sadness in response to the attack on the twin towers. That increased rhythm brought us together in a state of coherence for a brief window of time. As time passed and we resumed our lives, the rhythm went back to its normal flow. Following that experience, scientists went back and looked at other events. What they found is that it is not only tragedies which trigger a spike in the magnetic field. Events such as a Super Bowl can also affect it. The largest spike in the magnetic field of the earth occurred during the last episode of *"The Bachelor".* These events showed scientists that when we "feed" the magnetic field of the earth with coherent emotional experiences, it can impact a great number of people.

What does this mean? When groups of people collaborate to send coherent heart care to areas of unrest or suffering, it can help to reduce that unrest or suffering. Emotions not only create coherence or incoherence in our bodies but, like radio waves, also radiate outward and are detected by the nervous systems of others in our environment. It has been proven that a small group of people can actually impact larger numbers simply by focusing their thoughts. When the war between Lebanon and Israel began in 1982, researchers trained a group of people to feel peace in their bodies and to know they were at peace. These people were then positioned throughout the war torn areas of the Middle East. At the time they were feeling and knowing peace, terrorist activities ceased, crimes went down and even emergency room visits declined. When the feelings of the group changed, the situations were reversed. This confirmed that focused feelings by a group of people can impact conditions in the world around them. This study was known as the International Peace Project in the Middle East and results published in the Journal of Conflict Resolution in 1988. It even documents how many people are required to facilitate change. The magic number in a world of 6 billion is just under 8000. We are now a planet of 7 billion people. With the Internet, it is certainly possible to envision a group of 8000 or more people all feeling peace. What might that result be?

Many groups have been gathering together for several years now in prayer circles or to meditate and hold in consciousness the outcome of a particular event. They continue to this day. With the advent of the internet, all one needs to do is to type in a few key words, and you will be able to learn about these groups in a matter of seconds. *Common Passion* is a Global Social Collaborative of individuals and communities with a shared passion for compassion. They orchestrate global meditations and prayer events with all faith and wisdom traditions.

The Global Coherence Monitoring System is continuing to be developed and deployed. Thanks to advanced technology, the relationship between the electromagnetic waves generated in the earth's ionosphere and changes in the brain and nervous system can now be documented. The Global Coherence Monitoring system is currently measuring changes in the earth caused by emotions. There is a sensor sight in Saudi Arabia, and plans are to have 12 more sites. One of the major goals of the GCI is to study the effects of this and provide evidence of its validity.

The mission of the Global Coherence Initiative is to *unite people in heart focused care and intention, to facilitate the shift in global consciousness from instability and disease to balance, cooperation and enduring peace.* The GCI offers a full moon synchronized Care Focus each month. Participants from all over the world can virtually go into a Global Care Room and participate in the Care focus together; the time designated for this event is 4 am, 12 pm and 8 pm. There is a website to which you can go to determine the exact time the Care Focus will take place in your time zone. For more information on the Global Coherence Initiative, go to www.glcoherence.org

Lynn McTaggart is a well-known journalist and author. She has produced exhaustive research based on discoveries in the world of science, spirit and health. In her book, *The Intention Experiment*, Lynn cites research done by psychologist William Braud which suggested that while we can use intention for ourselves, we can also affect others. She believes that intention should be a highly specific aim or goal which one should visualize, using all five senses, as having already occurred. In her book *The Bond,* Lynn presents scientific evidence that we are all, indeed, connected from cells to societies. She shows that the essential impulse of life is a will to connect rather than a drive to compete and that our greatest desire is to help others. *"The Bond"* offers a breathtaking, visionary plan for a new way to live, in harmony with our true nature and with each other. I highly recommend it.

# *What's Next*

What's next? That's up to you. You will write the final chapter as we end one cycle and begin another. The Mayans predicted that, in this next 5125 year cycle, we will see humanity become more loving and compassionate. We will experience a peaceful era without war and we will begin to heal our planet. When we look at conditions in our world today, that prediction seems highly unlikely. However, Gregg Braden tells us that in his discoveries of ancient civilizations in many different areas, one thing is constant. There is no evidence in any of those civilizations of weapons or any sign that war occurred..

I believe the hearts of all human beings regardless of their ethnicity or "labels" respond with a heartbeat of love, caring and sharing. Love is more powerful than fear and much more powerful than hate. The year 2012 may be just the beginning of the birthing of a new Humanity.

On March 22, 2012, Barbara Marx Hubbard invited us to participate in "conception day" which she calls the conception of the birth of a new humanity which will be born on December 22, 2012. She described it as "supra-sex", the joining of our genius (rather than genes) to co-create a collective shift. Thousands of people joined in this event.

Everything we do or think affects our planet in some way. We are here on planet Earth at this time for a reason. Each of us can play a role in creating a future that is without war, hunger, violence, poverty or greed. We all must be evolutionary leaders. We can communicate with our dollars to support businesses that operate ethically and boycott businesses that do not. We can take the time to find out where the food we purchase comes from and how it is grown or produced. We can begin with ourselves, making just one change at a time that will benefit the environment and our neighbors. As we make changes in our own lives, it is reflected in our Universe. The energy of our hearts is the most powerful energy on the planet. Use it wisely, use it well and use it often!

You have read this book and hopefully used the internet to learn even more about some of the things you found most intriguing. Now you know the facts. There are no more excuses. Make the commitment now to become an Evolutionary Leader, a Cultural Creative, an Imaginal cell. Choose an area which speaks to your heart and find out how you can help to make the changes that are needed for us to become a new Humanity. Remember the words of John Lenin: "Imagine all the people, living life as one; you may think I'm a dreamer, but I'm not the only one." Today we can all wake up from that dream and make it a reality.

# *Conclusion*

It has been my intention to present the scientific facts as I have learned them with references to the experts and authors from whom I have read and learned. I hope I have peaked your interest and curiosity enough so that you will want to read the books I have recommended, visit the websites, do your own research and draw your own conclusions. I also hope you may be inspired to get involved in some way in helping to make this a healthier, more loving planet: a world that works for everyone.

If you are not a scientist (and I am not), these things may sound pretty strange. What we need to understand as we move forward with our lives is that the Universe is a vast and miraculous entity, and we are connected in ways we may have never dreamed. It is this connection that will make it possible for us to understand how to create a world of peace, harmony, health and joy for all.

We all have an ego. This is what gives us our personality and serves as a protective mechanism. We tend to believe that we are the most evolved species in the Universe, and that we will survive no matter what. But we have now learned that there were civilizations with technology at least as evolved as our own that existed thousands of years ago. What caused them to disappear?

Most of us pay little or no attention to what is happening beyond our planet in the Universe. Science has now shown us that we are connected to every other planet and star in this Universe and most probably other Universes still to be discovered. We know that new stars and planets are being discovered almost daily. We have learned that the alignment of planets, magnetism, and other phenomena occurring in the Universe does, indeed, affect planet Earth and its inhabitants. I urge you to use the internet to discover for yourself some of these remarkable studies that have caused scientists to change many of the beliefs that have been held true for so long. Look at your own beliefs and, with an open mind, entertain the idea that they may not be true today.

We have learned that there have been five mass extinctions, and that we are deep into the sixth. Gregg Braden, one of the greatest resources for this book, has stated that, as our planet makes its shift and we come to the end of a 5125 year cycle, those systems that are sustainable will thrive and those which are not will collapse. We have seen the collapse of our financial system and even our system of government does not seem to be working too well. We know we cannot continue to depend on non-renewable resources for energy. While some of us will delight in saying "I told you so" when discovering that we are not the cause of global warming, that does not mean we can continue to use our natural resources unwisely.

One of the discoveries science has made is that we are all truly connected. There is no "empty space". Everything we do or think affects another in some way. I think it is interesting that the Internet has emerged at this time, followed by Face Book, Twitter and other social media which keep us connected. We can now reach thousands of people at one time through teleconferences and e-mails. It is up to us to use them in a way which may inspire others to become more awake and aware of the changes taking place on Planet Earth. Many organizations have been doing this, and I encourage you to visit the website references listed in the back of this book. The computer is a perfect analogy for our Universe. The computer does not make decisions. It simply obeys the commands it receives from us. Sometimes it will ask us if we really want to do what we commanded with such messages as "do you really want to delete that?" I consider that the mind of the computer. The point is that, when you begin to use a computer, you realize how amazing it truly is and how much more you need to learn. The same is true of our Universe and the power it holds. Planet Earth is our home. However, our knowledge of this planet and the Universe is miniscule. Scientists and astrologers have long been curious and eager to learn about the space outside planet Earth. This has led to many discoveries. I would encourage you to become more aware of your home here on Earth. Are some of the changes that are occurring a message from the Universe? Think about it.

We've all heard that you can't solve problems with the same mind that created them. Yet, in all probability, we will attempt to solve many of the problems that we face today by doing the same thing and expecting different results. So, in order to truly make a change in our world, we need to move out of our minds and into our hearts. If someone proposes a solution that sounds outrageous, ridiculous, way out or impossible, think about what we knew just a few short years ago with regard to technology and what we know now. Think about what we believed about the Universe and our planet a few short years ago and what we now know. Things that were once thought to be "impossible" have been proven to be possible. How? Someone dared to imagine it. Fifty years ago, who could have imagined that we would see a human being walking on the moon? Who would have believed that you could send a piece of paper through a machine and, with the push of a button, have it arrive at a destination miles away? Cell phones and the internet were ideas that simply could not be comprehended. Today they are a part of our everyday life along with I-pads and kindles. How, then, can we discount the idea that all humanity on every part of this planet can live together in peace or that war will become a thing of the past? How do we know it is not possible to heal ourselves from disease?

As I was completing this book at the end of the year 2011, I thought it most fitting that the theme of the Rose Parade, 2012, was *Just Imagine.* Later on that day, I listened to an internet seminar with Dr. Phillip Zimbardo, Professor Emeritus of Psychology at Stanford University. He talked about the Heroic Imagination Project (HIP) that teaches people how to overcome the natural human tendency to watch and wait in moments of crisis. Their mission is to encourage and empower individuals to take heroic action during crucial moments in their lives. We have all seen many instances of heroic people who have risked their lives and performed what seemed like an impossible task to save someone's life. I invite you to visit the website at www.heroicimagination.com.

Every great invention or innovation has been conceived and created by someone just like you. In fact, everything, without exception, was created twice: first in the mind as an idea and then, by following through and taking action, it became form. These ideas, acted on and pursued by the innovator, have resulted in the amazing technology and way of life we enjoy today. Yet we can do better. Napoleon Hill said: "Whatever the mind of man can conceive and believe it can achieve." Those words were not uttered yesterday, but many yesterdays ago.

What breaks your heart? For me it is war. I firmly believe that war is unnecessary. Many years ago, the only way we could have light was with fire. Eons ago when our ancestors felt threatened, they used clubs or stones to protect themselves. As we progressed (and here I offer an editorial which would question that it was progress) we learned how to manufacture guns. Now the weapons we have at our disposal are capable of destroying an entire planet. For years, we have been spending trillions of dollars on high tech equipment designed to destroy whole communities and all of the people living there. We have sent hundreds of thousands of young men and women into battle in the name of security and freedom. And what has been the result? We still feel threatened and are under constant "alert". Thousands of young men and women have been killed, tearing apart marriages and leaving children without a mother or father. Still others return home maimed or crippled and often with severe mental and emotional problems.

It is time to change our thinking and ways of solving conflict here in America and around the world. It is possible, I believe, to help our neighbors across the planet live in peace without killing and bombs. There are those who proclaim the terrorists, aka the Taliban, can only be stopped by guns and bombs. I disagree. It's time to find another way. An organization that I have been involved with for the past few years is "The Peace Alliance". They are a group that is lobbying for HR808, a bill introduced in Congress to create a cabinet level Department of Peace. See www.thepeacealliance.org.

Hunger is another issue that breaks my heart. Think about this: seventeen thousand children die of starvation **each day** on our planet. Yet we produce more food globally than we could possible consume. Here's another fact for you. 1.2 billion people on our planet are underfed and malnourished. Conversely, another 1.2 billion people are overfed and suffering from health problems. In November, 2011 The Shift Network (referred in the back of this book) sponsored *The Food For All Summit*, an entire day that featured speakers from many organizations working to alleviate hunger. This was available to people all over the world via telephone and/or webcast. This is just one example of how we can gather people everywhere to work together to solve the problems of violence, hunger, homelessness and other issues that keep us from enjoying the life we deserve and desire. Many communities are creating "Hunger free zones". where people in need know they have a resource to get help. The HFC Network

(Hunger Free Communities Network) is a nationwide platform for coalitions, campaigns and collaborations committed to ending hunger in their localities, to learn from each other and share their knowledge and experience with other hunger-free organizers. The thing I find so remarkable about this organization is that it focuses on the local communities, each alleviating hunger one community at a time. This offers everyone an opportunity to be of service in his or her own community. Multiplied on a large scale, the end result could certainly be a world without hunger.

Are your schools a safe place for your children to learn or do you fear violence and bullying. If this is heartbreak for you, there are many organizations in place that have had success in dealing with and often eliminating these barriers to a safe education. One of them is Bully Safe Schools. They provide training, consultation and survey tools to help schools create and maintain safe physical and emotional climates.

Look around your neighborhood or community. Is there a problem that needs to be addressed? Are you part of the problem by complaining about it, or can you be part of the solution by stepping up to help? You might be surprised at the ideas that emerge from a group of committed citizens working together. Remember the words of Margaret Mead, "never doubt that a small group of thoughtful committed people can change the world; indeed, it is the only thing that ever has".

How can you use **your** expertise and talents to aid in making your family, community, nation and the world a better, safer, more peaceful place in which to live? If you are not sure how to contribute your specific talents, think about what you are most concerned about. Is it violence on our streets, our educational system, the environment, health care, our financial system, business practices, homelessness or hunger? I have listed many resources in this book, but I can tell you that there are literally thousands of organizations out there today addressing these issues and more. Use the internet to locate them and you will find a way to be of service.

Is there something you could do to make your community a better place? It may be as simple as picking up trash on the street or on the beach. It may be volunteering in one of your community organizations such as Meals on Wheels, the local animal shelter, Neighborhood Watch, a Boys and Girls Club or the Senior Center. It may be doing outreach within your spiritual community. Remember, you were put here on planet earth at this time for a reason. You can and must become an evolutionary leader, an imaginal cell.

Some changes need to be made through legislation. It could be on a local, state or national level. If there is something you are passionate about, write or call the appropriate legislator, senator or city council member. Send them an e-mail, fax or text. You might even telephone them. They are there to serve you! And they will listen. Be persistent but politely firm. Find groups that are lobbying for a change you believe in and support them. Submit a letter to your local newspaper with your concerns and perhaps even a solution. The problems of child abuse and spousal abuse, bullying, homelessness, hunger, and many other problems are being addressed by organizations in a positive, caring manner. Unfortunately, we don't hear much about these programs on the daily news. Does that disturb you? Contact your radio or TV station and express that concern. Don't support the advertisers on news programs that focus on violence and killing.

Remember that money talks! Many of the problems we face today are a result of greed and the competition for the dollar. The media will continue to produce what sells as will businesses and corporations. You can effect change. Show the powers that be how your idea will *save* money! Often the first objection to a new program is the cost. If we educate our young people in the early years to show kindness and respect to one another, we could spend less money on incarceration. If we sought a peaceful solution *first* to a world threat instead of gearing up our arms, how many millions of dollars might be saved from our "defense" budget? I know you can think of many more examples.

Our consciousness is always processing what we see, hear and think. Consider this: if the stories we hear on the nightly news are all about violence, murder and crime, what can we expect more of? If we continue to hear gloom and doom with regard to the economy or employment, what will we experience? If the stories we hear are about love, compassion, and heroism, can we expect more of this? Yes! There are many groups and individuals doing wonderful compassionate work around the globe. The nightly news overlooks these stories as they are not sensational enough to generate ratings. If it bleeds, it leads!

As with most every statement, there are exceptions. One of these is ABC World News with Diane Sawyer. Their series on "Made in America" has awakened not only consumers but businesses to the realization of how many of our everyday products are manufactured outside the United States. Many businesses are now rectifying this, and that will mean many more jobs which is one of our major concerns right now. As we consumers become aware of what we purchase and commit to spending just a few dollars on goods made in America, the resulting increase in jobs is seen immediately. Let me add here that in our global world we will not be competing for cheaper labor or the most exports or imports. "Made in America" will become "Made on planet Earth". As we share resources and ideas, goods and services will be produced in a way which will benefit all of humanity. However, we must take care of ourselves (America) first in order to be better equipped to lead the way. Remember the airlines mandate: "Put your mask on first, then assist your child". As I was completing the writing of this book during the Christmas season, ABC World News also shared stories of people visiting the layaway departments of stores and anonymously paying for the merchandise for a perfect stranger.

I believe there is more good occurring on our planet today than bad. I also believe there are individuals who understand where our evolution must take us if we are to survive and create a world free of hatred, violence, poverty, war and scarcity. These individuals are knowledgeable and creative souls who know how to solve some of the problems contributing to the demise of the planet. You may be one of them. You can become an evolutionary leader, a cultural creative and, yes, an imaginal cell. Don't just think about what might be done. Do something about it. The first step is to visit some of the websites I have listed. Read the books. It will become clear to you what your contribution might be.

Bruce Lipton says that the analogy of the butterfly is perfect for where we are in our own evolution right now. When a caterpillar begins the process of metamorphosis, everything breaks down and it appears that the organism is dying. However, **one cell** (the imaginal cell) then does something "different" and begins the evolution into the perfection and beauty of a butterfly. The process of metamorphosis is usually accompanied by a change in habitat or behavior. Many of our current systems are breaking down including our economic system, health care and even our way of government. The behavioral changes needed for us to become a "butterfly" may seem outrageous, difficult and even ridiculous. Continuing on our present path with our current behavior is even more ridiculous.

We, here on planet earth, are about to give birth to a new humanity. Barbara Marx Hubbard calls it "Birth 2012", with conception being March 22, 2012 and the "due date" December 21. I believe we have been in a 5125 year "gestation" period, and what will emerge on December 21 and beyond will be the connection of 7 plus billion cells uniting in a new humanity.

I hope you may be inspired to take action in some way and/or pass this book on to a friend. Just as each cell in our body has a specific purpose, so, too, each of us, as a cell in the body of humanity, has a specific purpose. (Bruce Lipton, *Spontaneous Evolution)* One of our main jobs is to discover who we are and why we are here. There are no two human beings exactly alike and each of us has a talent that no one else has.

You will hear many spiritual leaders talk about how we are living in the most important and incredible time ever. There has never been a time in history that we have faced so many challenges of such great magnitude at the same time. We are here for a reason. We are here to co-create a world built with love: a world without war, violence, hunger or homelessness. We all have areas that spark our interest and in which we excel. That is the place to begin. Our evolution must come from the inside out. It must begin with each of us awakening to the fact that we can do better, and make a commitment to be the change we want to see. If changing the world seems impossible, consider this: Because we are all connected, whenever one person changes something within themselves, it produces a ripple effect and makes it easier for others to change.

Let there be peace on Earth and let it begin with me" is a song I have loved and sung hundreds of times with many groups of people. Peace, love, kindness, prosperity and joy must begin with ourselves before we can extend it to others. When it does and when we do extend it, the possibilities are endless! The time is now. The choice is yours. There are no limits to what we can create when we get out of our minds and into our hearts. Will we continue in a downward spiral doing the same thing over and over again or will we wake up and realize that major changes are needed now? Extinction or evolution… Crisis or creation: it's up to you.

# *References*

The references listed here are intended to give you more complete information about the shift that is happening on our planet, what it means and how you might lend your personal talents in creating a world that works for everyone. At the very least, you will have an eye-opening experience reading any of these books.

## <u>BOOKS</u>

*Hope*, by Andrew Harvey:*A long awaited compelling guide that helps people respond to current global challenges yet also serves as a much needed wake-up call to inspire action through sacred activism.*

*The Bond,* by Lynn McTaggart: *A breathtaking, visionary plan for a new way to live, in harmony with our true nature and with each other, and a new way to heal our relationships, our neighborhoods and our world.*

*The Intention Experiment,* by Lynn McTaggart: *Using Your Thoughts to Change Your Life and the World*

*The Field*, by Lynn McTaggart: **The Quest For the Secret Force of the Universe**

*Spontaneous Evolution*, by Bruce Lipton and Steve Bhaerman: **A new and hopeful story about humanity's evolutionary destiny**

*The Biology of Belief*, By Bruce Lipton: **a groundbreaking work in the field of new biology showing that our bodies can be changed as we retrain our thinking.**

*Fractal Time*, by Gregg Braden: **a powerful model of time and a realistic window into what we can expect for the mysterious year 2012 and beyond**

*The Divine Matrix,* by Gregg Braden: **Bridging time, space, miracles and belief**

*Deep Truth:* by Gregg Braden: **Igniting the Memory of Our Origin, History, Destiny, and Fate**

*A New Earth,* by Eckhart Tolle: **Awakening to Your Life's Purpose**

*The Mystery of 2012: Predictions, Prophecies and Possibities:* a collection of essays by many contributors

*The shift,* by Wayne Dyer: **Taking your life from ambition to meaning**

*When Hope Takes a Stand*: John and Ocean Robbins

*Jump Time*, by Jean Houston: **shaping your future in a world of radical change**

*Aware, Awake, Alive*, by Dr. Elliott S. Dacher, M.D.: **bringing together the wisdom and practices of East and West, introducing the reader to a time-tested, practical and accessible approach to a far-reaching health and healing.**

*The Living Universe: Where Are We? Who Are We? Where Are We Going?* by Duane Elgin. Other books by Duane Elgin: **Promise Ahead: A Vision of Hope and Action for Humanities Future; Awakening Earth: Exploring the Evolution of Human Culture and Consciousness. Voluntary Simplicity: Toward a Way of Life that is Outwardly Simple, Inwardly Rich.**

*I Believe: When What You Believe Matters:* by Eldon Taylor

*A Mindful Nation*: Congressman Tim Ryan

*The Better World Shopper Guide and The Better World Handbook*: by Dr. Ellis Jones; A comprehensive guide for socially and environmentally responsible consumers, ranking products A to F

## OTHER RESOURCES

The teachings and programs offered by these organizations were a major motivation for the writing of this book. I became fascinated with what I was hearing and wanted to share this information with everyone! I invite you to visit their websites and learn for yourself.

**The Shift Network:** Stephen Dinan, CEO
www.theshiftnetwork.com

Stephen Dinan is the CEO of the Shift Network and member of the prestigious Transformational Leadership Council and Evolutionary Leaders groups. As the former director of membership and marketing at the Institute of Noetic Sciences, he was the driving force behind the shift in action program which grew to 10,000 paying members and the One Minute Shift video series which was seen by more than one million. He is also the author of *"Radical Spirit"* (New World Library) and a forthcoming book *Sacred America*. Stephen directed and helped to create the Esalen's Institute Center for Theory and Research, a think tank for leading scholars, researchers and teachers to explore human potential frontiers. The Shift Network was launched in February 2010. Their aim is to empower a global movement of people who are creating an evolutionary shift of consciousness that in turn leads to a more enlightened society; one built on principles of sustainability, peace, health and prosperity. Now is the time for an upgrade to our planetary operating system. Go to http:// vision 2012plan.com to see the big picture of what this organization envisions for the future. The Shift Network has designated the seasons of 2012 depicting our evolution into a new way of living on the planet and a new humanity: they are:

- Winter of wellness
- Spring of Sustainability
- Summer of Peace
- Autumn of abundance

Each season will feature speakers and programs designed to offer ways to design a future of wellness, sustainability peace and abundance for the planet.

### The Shift Network: Birth 2012

The Shift Network has brought together many of the world's most knowledgeable and enlightened spiritual teachers who offer their teachings via the internet. One of the most exciting programs that I have discovered is ***Birth 2012***, Synergy Day. We know that December 21, 2012 marks the end of a cycle of 5125 years of the Mayan calendar and the beginning of a new cycle. Predictions surrounding this transition revolve around change, particularly a shift from separateness to oneness and moving from conflict and dissention to peace and harmony. To celebrate this transition, The Shift Network has collaborated with many spiritual teachers and leaders who will lead a momentous event called ***Birth 2012***.

Barbara Marx Hubbard, visionary, social pioneer and author has put forth this exciting and hopeful vision called Birth 2012. She encourages us to declare an actual "birth date" signifying a new era of human evolution. The global birthday celebration will occur on December 22, 2012. On March 22, 2012, Barbara, along with the Shift Network, celebrated *Global Conception Day*, symbolically nine months before the "birth". On this day, each of us was invited to "inseminate" into the collective our own ideas and visions of what we believe can be born. To make this event "fun", the Shift Network will be issuing "birth certificates" to those making a commitment to be born as a Global Citizen. You can join with these respected thought leaders and teachers and be a part of this transformational shift. I invite and encourage you to visit the website at www.birth2012.com to learn how you can be a part of this celebration.

In celebrating the birth of a new era, we recognize December 21, 2012 as the passing away of the old; systems and ideas that no longer serve us. On December 22, 2012, we celebrate the activation of the new and identify what is being born. We give our gifts, not to the baby being born, but to each other in celebration and participation in a new humanity.

### The Global Coherence Initiative
www.glcoherence.org

A collaborative research project with the Institute of HeartMath. The mission of the GCI is science based co-creative projects to unite people in heart focused care and intention, to facilitate the shift in global consciousness from instability and disease to balance, cooperation and enduring peace. When large numbers of people respond to a global event with a common emotional feeling, the collective response can affect the activity in the earth's field. Emotions not only create coherence or incoherence in our bodies but, like radio waves, also radiate outward and are detected by the nervous systems of others in our environment.

**Institute of Heartmath:** Doc Childre, founder; Howard Martin, EVP
www.heartmath.org.

The Institute of Heart Math has as its mission to help establish heart based living and global coherence by inspiring people to connect with the intelligence and guidance of their heart. Heart Math is a system, one minute techniques to connect with intelligence of the heart and reach a higher level of thinking. Heart is the new intelligence. It is reached by the flow of awareness that we experience once the mind and bodily emotions are brought into balance, resulting in coherence.

**The Peace Alliance:** Matthew Albrecht
www.thepeacealliance.org

This group was formed to lobby for a bill to create a cabinet level Department of Peace. The bill was authored by Dennis Cucinich and has been introduced in Congress at least three times. There are groups throughout the United States working to educate people about the bill and encourage them to contact their Representative and ask for his or her support of the bill.

**Integral Institute:** Ken Wilbur and Roger Walsh
www.integralinstitute.org

This institute aims to help solve the world's most complex problems using a comprehensive integral and non-partial approach. Among the issues are global warming, evolutionary forms of capitalism and the culture wars in political, religious and scientific domains.

**Integral Spiritual Practice**: Terry Patton: founder and a vital leading voice in the emerging fields of integral evolutionary leadership and spirituality

**Beyond Awakening:** Terry Patten, host of a series of conversations with many of today's most dynamic spiritual teachers.

**The ReCreation Foundation,Inc.** is a non-profit foundation created by Neale Donald Walsch to address the overwhelming response from people around the world who desire to do something tangible to spread the message of Conversations with God. The Vision of The ReCreation Foundation is a planet where world peace and global sustainability is a reality.

**Quantum Healing Consciousness and Soul**: Shifra Hendrie

Quantum Healing and Soul is a project of the Gate of Unity and Kabbalah of Transformation, whose mission is to transform our world through illuminating the minds, hearts, souls and lives of people around the globe with the divine wisdom of authentic Kabbalah.

**McClean Masterworks**: The Art of Life Mastery: Jennifer McLean, CEO and host of **Healing with the Masters:** a series of inspirational speakers and videos. Jennifer's goal is to act as a conduit and amplifier to share her and others' sacred inspirations and visions on a large scale to encourage and empower shifts in perception for increased global consciousness.

**The Masters Gathering:** The Ultimate Transformation Experience: Harrison Klein, host and founder and Farhana Dhalla, co-host. A series of transformational speakers.

**The Aware Show**: Lisa Garr: The Aware Show is dedicated to communicating information that inspires positive growth and change. The goal is increased an awareness and healing on an individual and planetary level. Broadcast every Wednesday and Thursday at 1pm in Los Angeles on KPFK (90.7 fm)

**Youwealth Revolution:** Darius Barazandeh: The Youwealth Revolution is a global virtual training conference and intention event, featuring the world's leading inspirational change agents, wealth creators, authors and teachers. Their purpose is to awaken millions to connect with their inner wealth, passion and purpose and create the amazing and inspired life they so richly deserve.

**Evolving Wisdom**: www.evolvingwisdom.com

This organization is committed to serving the evolution of consciousness and culture on the planet by building and nurturing a global transformative learning community that brings visionaries and wisdom teachers together with passionate learners for the purpose of creating deep transformation at all levels.

**Evolve 2012 Initiative:** Natan Lev, host
www.evolve2012initiative.com

This organization has as its mission to create a multi-dimensional conversation that supports the needs of individuals, small businesses and organizations as well as the emerging community of evolutionary entrepreneurs and the new social and economic infrastructure that will support our individual and collective growth.

**Duane Elgin:** Duane Elgin, MBA and MA, is an internationally recognized speaker, author and social visionary who looks beneath the surface turbulence of our times to explore the deeper trends that are transforming our world. In 2006, Duane received the Japanese "Goi International Peace Award" in recognition of his contribution to a global 'vision, consciousness and lifestyle' that foster a more sustainable and spiritual culture.

**Kickstart.org:** Founded by Martin Fisher, CEO and Nick Moon, Managing Director Kickstart has as its mission to get millions of people out of poverty quickly, cost effectively and sustainably. Their five step program is to 1)Identify opportunities 2) Design products 3) Establish a supply chain 4) Develop the Market and 5) Measure and move along. To date 17,800 jobs have been created and 121,400 enterprises have been created. At this time, their work is centered primarily in Kenya, Tanzania and Mali.

**Living Economies Forum:** formerly People Centered Development Forum; David Korten, author, lecturer, engaged citizen:"The old economy of greed and dominion is dying; a new economy of life and partnership is struggling to be born. The outcome is ours to choose."

**We, the World:** (www.WE.net) a Global campaign to unite and amplify the efforts of people, organizations and movements working for the common good.

**Enlighten Next:** Founded by Andrew Cohen in 1988; dedicated to catalyzing evolution in consciousness and culture.

www.ingramcontent.com/pod-product-compliance
Lightning Source LLC
Chambersburg PA
CBHW020337290526
45785CB00005B/2053